Epic Trips

of

The West

❖

Tom Stienstra's
Ten Best

Foghorn
Press

BOOKS BUILDING COMMUNITY™

ISBN 0-935701-83-4

Epic Trips

of

The West

❖

Tom Stienstra's
Ten Best

Foghorn Press
BOOKS BUILDING COMMUNITY

Book Credits

Managing Editor—*Ann-Marie Brown*
Assistant Editors—*Samantha Trautman, Howard Rabinowitz*
Book Design and Layout—*Ann-Marie Brown, Michele Thomas*
Cover Design—*I. Magnus*

Photo Credits

pp. 5, 8, 22, 33, 92, 140—Jeffrey Patty
p. 36—Jim McDaniel
p. 39—Steve Essaf
p. 56—Bob Roberts
p. 63—Jeron Drew
p. 72—John Reginato
p. 73—Bobbi Wolverton
p. 76—Angelo Cuanang
p. 88—Abe Cuanang
pp. 116, 129—Kurt Rogers
p. 130—John Storey
pp. 146, 152, 188, 192, 194, 197—Tom Stienstra
pp. 158, 164—Katy Raddatz
p. 182—Trevor Slaymaker

Acknowledgments

Special thanks to Will Hearst, Jim Sevrens, Phil Bronstein,
Glenn Schwarz, Rick Nelson, Kevin Casey,
Charles Cooper and the late Dave Halvorsen
of the *San Francisco Examiner.*

About the Author

Tom Stienstra is the outdoors writer for the *San Francisco Examiner*, which distributes his column nationally on the Scripps News Service. He was named California Outdoor Writer of the Year in 1990 and 1992, and is currently serving as a director of the Outdoor Writers Association of America.

Other books by Tom Stienstra:
California Camping
California Fishing
California Hiking (with Michael Hodgson)
Pacific Northwest Camping
Rocky Mountain Camping (with Robyn Schlueter)
Great Outdoor Getaways to the Bay Area and Beyond
Careers in the Outdoors

To the Reader:

Is there really a Bigfoot? What of man-eating sharks that bark like dogs and bite off propellers? Can modern men and women stand up to the challenges faced by the Voyageurs of the Hudson Bay Company?

What is it like to walk on America's highest trail in the footprints of Muir, Whitney and Brewer? Can rafters survive one of the West's wildest rivers at flood stage? What do you do when you're fighting a giant trout and a grizzly emerges from the bush to charge you?

Take a hard look at this book and you'll find some answers to these questions. Plus, you'll have the chance to travel with me on some of the greatest expeditions in North America's wildest regions.

It has been part of my job as an outdoors writer to seek out the West's epic trips—destinations ranging from Mount Whitney in California to Great Bear Lake in the Arctic Circle and anywhere in between. My goal was to take my readers with me every step of the way, up close and personal, so everyone could share in the exhilaration of these rare and fantastic outdoor experiences. The result is this book, a compilation of 10 expeditions that run the spectrum of the wild outdoors.

Hope you enjoy reading them as much as I enjoyed doing them...

—Tom Stienstra

Table of Contents

❖

Heading off into the Siskiyou Wilderness in search of Bigfoot

The Search for
BIGFOOT

Tracking the Legend in Northern California & Oregon

❖

The snowfield stretched out before us for a hundred yards, and though reflected sunlight made us shield our eyes, the huge footprints could not be mistaken: 17 inches long! Six inches wide! Bigfoot? Or fakes?

We were silent, just standing there, staring at them. Each of these massive prints plunged 10 inches deep into the snow, and where each one bottomed out, the snow was rock hard from being packed down. Whatever made these prints, it was big and heavy—but it was not a bear. The steps followed in an even one-two, one-two through the snow, the trail from a two-legged creature.

The Bigfoot Expedition, a project that entailed more than six months of extensive research and a month in the field, had led us to the Klamath Mountains northeast of Eureka, and now to these footprints. As we looked closer, I remembered what Grover Kranz, an anthropology professor and Bigfoot specialist, said about a set of footprints that provides the best evidence yet for the existence of Bigfoot.

"We've got over 1,000 cases of sightings and plaster casts of prints," Kranz said. "But now we have ones with dermal ridges and that's what sets them apart. The intricate pattern of skin ridges would be almost impossible even for the best hieroglyphics expert to fake. I am convinced Bigfoot exists."

Dutch geologist Ral von Koenigswald came across a number of unusual human-like teeth, including a lower molar that was twice the size of the corresponding tooth in an adult gorilla. An unusual jawbone was found in China by Dr. Pei Wen-chung. He identified it as belonging to a descendant of Gigantopithecus. Bigfoot? Or fakes?

We're talking about a man-like beast who stands eight feet tall and weighs 800 pounds, leaves little trace of his presence save his giant footprints, and has confounded explorers for thousands of years in remote areas around the world. The descendant of Gigantopithecus has been called by many names: the Abominable Snowman of Mt. Everest, the Yeti of China, the Sasquatch of British Columbia, the Mono Grande of the Andes and Russia's Agachikishi. In the Klamath Mountains, the Hupa Indians call him *Ohmahah,* which means Wild Man of the Woods. In the past century, trailblazers and loggers have called him Bigfoot, and the name has stuck.

We were searching for him. My partners were both wilderness explorers: photographer Jeffrey Patty and U.S. Forest Service scientist Michael Furniss. The three of us traveled light and quick over some of the most rugged and remote terrain in California and Oregon, exploring key areas where Bigfoot sightings and tracks had been most prevalent. We hiked mountain rims, bushwhacked into dense wilderness, crossed through streams chilled by glacial melt and, at times, even crawled on hands and knees on animal trails to reach areas rarely, if ever, visited by anyone.

Our first trip was mapped to take us into the Siskiyou Wilderness, a diverse habitat filled with firs, pines, spruces and cedars, and cut by a vast spiderweb of mountain streams. After traveling via four-wheel drive on a logging road to the Bear Basin Saddle at 4,900 feet, we found the road blocked by snow.

"This is where we start doing some thumpin' and gruntin,'" said Patty, gazing to the north at the Siskiyou Backbone, a long series of jagged mountain crests, all covered by snow. "Maybe it's time for me to start using the Bigfoot call I've been working on."

Furniss and I looked at him as if he had antlers growing out of his head. The scream of Bigfoot is allegedly an intense, cackling shriek that cannot be imitated without electronic equipment.

"Let's hear it," I said.

Patty put his hands to his mouth, then shouted across the canyon, "Here Bigfoot, Bigfoot. Heeere Bigfoot."

When we crossed the first snowfield, the unbroken surface told us just what we wanted to know. "This area has not been open to vehicular traffic all winter," said Furniss. "There are no footprints at all in the snow, so that means we are the first people to walk into this part of the wilderness area in months, maybe in half a year, maybe more."

That was a critical factor in our trip, and why we had been so secretive about the areas we intended to explore—we didn't want to get duped by a hoaxter. Like the mysteries of Unidentified Flying Objects, ghosts and the Bermuda Triangle, a mystique surrounds Bigfoot's existence as well. It can set people off in the woods wearing gorilla costumes, using stamps to make footprints. Bigfoot can lead to bizarre tales.

For instance, an Oregon man who would not allow the use of his name said that he watched Bigfoot get out of a spaceship, and then talked to him. "I also saw the Little People," he said, dead serious. A commercial fisherman at Moss Landing—who also wouldn't provide his name—said he knew why no Bigfoot carcasses had been found. "The Bigfoot go to sea to die," he said. "I just saw one swimming in Monterey Bay." Well, the Bigfoot we were looking for did not have a zipper running down his back.

Only Terry Moyles, the primate specialist at San Francisco Zoo, had knowledge of the areas we were exploring. Having heard of our expedition, Moyles called us and suggested two areas. Remarkably, those were two of the five areas we had already targeted after six months of research.

It was Patty's idea to occasionally retrace our trail to see if, indeed, Bigfoot would be tracking us instead of the other way around. So after three days of wilderness travel, we decided to hike back to inspect a series of snowfields. If anything was following us, it would show up in the snow.

It was an all-day pull, a warm June day where snow can melt rapidly. Late in the afternoon, we broke through some trees and found the snowfield. What we saw was hard to believe. Here were these giant footprints staring at us, carving an icy trail around the bend. They seemed awesome, and the blinding reflection of light off the snow added to the mystery. I measured one—17 inches long!

Furniss, the scientist, looked at me with apprehension and said, "Nobody's going to believe this."

The trip was just three days old. Were we already close to Mr. Bigfoot? We kept staring and measuring, but something seemed amiss. We all sensed it at once.

"I don't think this is Bigfoot," Patty said. "The footprints don't seem far enough apart." Sure enough, the distance between them was only 17 or 18 inches. That is about the stride of a man who is 6-foot-1. Well, that's how tall I am. Then I tried walking in the footprints. Perfect match, except for the outrageous size.

Then it hit us. The footprints were our own, created on the way in when each of us stepped in the same spot to ease the travel across soft snow. But 17 inches? Figure it: The hot early days of summer had melted the snow on the edge of the footprints, turning the print of a 13-inch hiking boot into a 17-inch Bigfoot print.

That night, in our sleeping bags at camp, we were watching the stars, talking about the day's episode. Saturn, the Big Dipper and Polaris patrolled the sky.

Furniss spotted a shooting star, then spoke quietly. "I'm a scientist and I'm trained in logic, but there are things for which there is no rational explanation," he said. "I guess Bigfoot falls into that territory."

Logic gives us what we need, but magic gives us what we crave.

Michael Furniss snapped his head as if somebody had jerked him up by the hair. "There's something up there," he shouted, pointing at the high, snow-flecked terrain across a steep canyon.

For the single flash of a moment, I caught a glimpse of a large furry creature walking on two legs, perhaps seven feet tall, disappearing into the woods some two miles distant. Then there was nothing but stillness. We stared at the mountain, searching for any movement.

"Probably not Bigfoot," Furniss said, but he didn't sound so convinced.

He grabbed the binoculars and scoped the mountain. "Nothing now," he said, but he continued to probe, waiting. We decided to set up a watch.

This was in the Siskiyou Wilderness—Bigfoot Country—near Devil's Punchbowl. It is remote country, and judging by the complete lack of hiker tracks in the snowfields we had crossed, we were the first to explore the area that year.

These mountains are filled with mysteries and magic. One of the earliest documented Bigfoot sightings recorded occurred near there on January 2, 1886, and was reported in the now defunct *Del Norte Record.* "Mr. Jack Dover, one of our most trustworthy citizens," the account reads, "saw an object standing 150 yards from him picking berries or tender shoots from the bushes. The thing was of gigantic size—about seven feet high—with a bulldog head, short ears and long hair. He aimed his gun at the animal, or whatever it was, several times, but because it was so human, would not shoot."

Similar sightings have been repeated in these mountains hundreds of times this century. The key here is the habitat. The Klamath and Siskiyou ranges have a remarkable variety of trees and plants, which support a wide variety of animals. Beyond past reports of strange sightings of giant creatures here, that variety was a critical factor in why we selected the area for part of the expedition. "It is an established fact that this area has the greatest density of conifers in one place anywhere in the world," Furniss said. The area also has the food, water and remoteness Bigfoot would demand.

One of the best examples is between Trout Camp and Wilderness Falls at Clear Creek, where the bedrock alternates from granite to peridotite, just the habitat changes we had been searching for. "Granite gives rise to a tan, sandy soil that grows an abundance of vegetation, grasses and trees," Furniss said. "Peridotite gives rise to a red soil, impoverished, that supports a more slow-growing, sparse-looking flora."

It is on these edges of habitat, where granite and peridotite meet, where wildlife is often abundant and varied, and where Bigfoot might make his home. In a 30-minute span, we saw footprints from bear, deer and mountain lion, as well as a small pocket of water next to a meadow, mysteriously muddied. From what?

"Some kind of animal has been playing in it," observed Furniss. Bigfoot? In the movie *Bigfoot*, there is supposed documentary footage of an alleged Bigfoot playing in such a puddle. However, the Bigfoot looked suspiciously like a man in a costume.

While tales of a giant beast are relatively common in remote areas of the Pacific Northwest, the Himalayas, and even in the Soviet Union, the Klamath/Siskiyou mountains are one of the few places in the world where the creature is reputed to have shown an occasional tendency toward violence. One such episode was recorded in 1890 in the little-known book, *The Hermit of Siskiyou*, in which a bizarre tale was reported from a logging camp:

"One morning, our guards failed to come in for breakfast," the account reads. "That ain't like a logging man. We went out to look. The poor souls had been picked up like firewood and slammed against those big tree trunks. We armed ourselves and followed the tracks. We had no doubt that old Bigfoot had murdered them. We followed his trail far into the Siskiyou Mountains, and finally lost it in some volcanic rocks."

Truth or fiction? Tales of old-time mountain men have a way of plying fiction with truth. For instance, even the great Davy Crockett claimed to have escaped an attack from the Spanish army by riding a bear down a waterfall. Such are the stories of some mountain men. Regardless, the stories of Bigfoot attacks in the Siskiyous are often told, and a good many people up here believe them.

It is the violence factor that led some to question our sanity for not bringing any kind of gun along, say a .45-caliber handgun, which can provide ideal protection in the woods. Why not bring a gun? The answer lies in Bigfoot's alleged sensory abilities, his ability to detect the smell of gun powder, oil and metal, which has a distinct scent.

"We can theorize that Bigfoot lives by his nose," said Jeff Patty. "To a large extent, his nose is his brain. The forest is dense, and I personally doubt the creature's eyesight is so amazing, since it would rarely need remarkable eyesight. Its sense of smell, on the other hand, is probably so developed that it is as if we, in comparison, do not even have noses. Even the hint of gunpowder, given Bigfoot's intelligence, and it's good-bye. You'll never see him." It is for this reason, Patty believes, that Bigfoot has never been hunted down and shot—and never will be. So we stood by our decision to travel without any guns.

And now, across the canyon, high on the mountain, we had seen a glimpse of a large creature, similar to the description of Bigfoot. At daybreak, we set up a watch, keeping the binoculars trained on the area where we had seen it. The brief glimpse the evening before had made me nervous.

It was my turn at the watch, and I dropped the binoculars and just gazed at the wonder of this country for a few minutes. A glacial peak towered above the canyon, its sides covered with fir and pines. The only noise was the rustling from a light breeze in the treetops.

Just then, out of nowhere on that mountain slope, I saw a movement about two miles distant. I looked closer with the binoculars, and then a dark shape emerged in a clearing.

I was so excited that the binoculars banged off my eyebrows, then sighted and focused in on the creature. "What is it?" whispered Furniss.

When you're on an expedition like we were, you expect to see things. Big things with big feet. I would have settled for kind of big feet, or even the man in the Bigfoot costume from the movie.

But it was just Smokey the Bear, making his morning rounds.

"Crunch-crunch, crunch-crunch."

The noise snapped us to attention.

"Did you hear that?" asked Furniss, in a tone scarcely audible. I nodded, listening for even the slightest sound. "Something's out there for sure."

We were at a meadow a few hundred feet above Clear Creek, and had noticed some sort of animal trail that appeared to lead down to the stream—which also bisected the animal trail we were following. Something was out there, heading to the stream on the animal trail, and it was going to run right into us.

"Crunch-crunch, crunch-crunch." It was getting closer.

"It's got to be Mr. Bear," said Furniss, sounding as if he was trying to convince himself as much as Patty and I. "But it doesn't sound much like Mr. Bear."

Indeed it didn't. It sounded like two distinct footsteps, one-two, one-two. Nobody said it, but we all thought it. Bigfoot? When we were quiet, it was quiet. When we moved, it moved. This went on for 10 minutes.

"Maybe we should throw a rock out there and find out what it is," suggested Furniss. But an instant later, he thought otherwise: "Throw a rock and we may not want to know what it is. It could be something that could throw something bigger right back at us."

In this same relative area, in August of 1958, a timber operation was invading the wilderness with the construction of a logging road. Supposedly, an unknown visitor made a late-night appearance at the road builder's camp. An oil drum was carried up a slope and tossed into a ravine. An 800-pound tire and wheel were lifted from an earth mover and dumped 50 yards away. The only clue to the prowler's identity were huge footprints found around the equipment. Plaster casts made by archeologists from the prints have never been proven to be fakes. This episode ran through my mind as we tried to discern any sound from the woods. We listened, but there was nothing, not even a snapping twig, no hint of anything.

"If it left, it sure left mighty quiet," said Jeff Patty.

We headed for the area, poking through the forest where the sound seemed to originate from, but found nothing. No footprints. No more sounds. No bear grunts, no shrieking Bigfoot calls. Nothing. We moved on, more mystified than ever.

The day heated up, and big drops of sweat poured off Patty's nose onto the map, splattering like rain drops. But there was no rain, not with 100-degree temperatures. We had arrived at Clear Creek, an untouched stream in the wilderness interior.

"No way around it," said Patty, all 6-foot-5 of him drenched in perspiration after four hours of heavy hoofin'. "This map don't lie. We have to ford this stream."

Even though the sun was like a branding iron, creeping our way hip-deep through a stream filled with 38-degree glacial melt was hardly an enticing proposition. But our intent was to explore rarely-visited areas—where Bigfoot may lurk—and that demanded searching out animal trails, bushwhacking into wilderness and crossing icy rivers.

"I'll go first," said Furniss. When his legs dipped into the stream, his face screwed up tight from the icy water. Five steps later, he was smiling. "Hey, it's not so cold anymore!" he shouted.

"That's because his legs are already numbed out from that icy water," Patty said with a grin.

Furniss took a few more tentative steps, then started to teeter where the stream was swiftest. He pressed hard with the tree limb he was using as a wading staff, trying to balance himself, but he started to tip. Right then the current dumped him, tumbling him in the near-freezing water.

"Yow!" he shouted, managing to scramble to the opposite bank. "I'm wet and cold, but okay."

Patty and I followed, the icy water nearly paralyzing our legs, but we crossed just the same.

A bit later, in the midst of a light descent on the way to Wilderness Falls, Jeff began lightly singing a song we had written while hiking in:

He's a mountain man, he's an old mountain man.
Kicking trail, every day he can.
Wilderness calls to him.
Meadows, streams and the mountain rims.

Furniss smiled. Sure, he went for a little swim, but he had rediscovered the magic of the outdoors. The idea is to get out there on the edge, and sometimes, when you go over the edge, you find out it's an amazing and exhilarating place to be.

Wilderness Falls, 10 miles away, beckoned us with three stream crossings and bushwhacks with no trail. With the heat, your eyes can sting from the salt in your sweat dripping from your forehead. Your clothes feel sticky, like a coating of wet glue. The heat drains the vitamins right out of you. To supplement our light diet, we were taking calcium and magnesium tablets, vitamin C and vitamin B. Those you can buy. For a light breeze I gladly would've paid $100, but the wilderness wasn't selling.

But the wild creatures up there didn't seem to mind. We were hiking just under the snow line—where the ground was being exposed to sun for the first time that year. Although spring was long past in warmer climates, it was just emerging here. Around us, everything was thriving. A red plant was erupting out of the ground, a snowflower. Alongside it were Indian paintbrush, azaleas, trillium. Butterflies were hatching and snakes were lying on rocks, trying to shake off the long winter's cold.

We hiked on, Furniss setting the pace, and then off in the distance, we could hear a faint crashing of water. We rounded a bend, jumped over some boulders and spotted the bubbling tower of water. Wilderness Falls, created by Clear Creek, seems to have two stages, first crashing down 45 feet into a boulder, then pounding its way into a foaming pool about 100 feet across.

Furniss and I were sitting atop a boulder at its head, the spray like a cold shower.

"What do you suppose that noise was in the woods?" I asked him.

"Just don't know," he said. "Didn't see it, no tracks, no grunts." You figure it.

From Canyon Peak lookout, we could see more than 100 square miles of Oregon wildlands, all so quiet that even a soft voice seemed an intrusion. Nobody was there, and nobody had been there for a long, long time.

Somewhere in the basin below, where giant cedars are like studs among a lush undergrowth, some men say Bigfoot walks. Maybe two, maybe many. We'd settle for one. After a day of traipsing our way into the interior of the Kalmiopsis Wilderness in Oregon, we were setting up camp when a bizarre sound blew a big hole in the silence. It was as if somebody was thumping a hollow log with a drumstick: "Thump, thump, thump, thump, thump." Five times. It echoed in the forest.

The next evening, just as I was stoking the campfire, it came again. "Thump, thump, thump, thump, thump." Again, five times.

"What's that?" asked Patty, a fellow well schooled in the sounds of the wild.

I shook my head. I had never heard it before. But we both knew it was far from the cackling shriek reputed to be the cry of Bigfoot.

Those who claim to have heard the wild cry of Bigfoot have the look of wonderment in their eyes when they talk of it. Like the scream itself, such a look cannot be imitated. Joe Eudemiller, a respected gent who owns a fine restaurant, has the look. "We (he

and his wife) were driving across Alaska and one night we were in
the trailer and heard this terrible scream, this incredibly frightful
scream like nothing we had ever heard in the world," said
Eudemiller, his eyebrows raising. "Whatever it was, it came up to
my trailer and shook it, violently. We were afraid for our lives. Then
we heard it again, many times through the night. It was a piercing
cry. After daylight, I went outside and found these huge crimps in
the top of the trailer—thick steel—where the thing had gripped it
when it shook us."

The reports of maniacal screams and strange noises in the
Oregon wilderness southwest of Grants Pass are one reason why
author Gerald DiPego chose this area as the setting for the novel
Shadow of the Beast, a fictional search for Bigfoot. By the book's end,
a lone female anthropologist has discovered Bigfoots all over the
place, while the other members of the expedition have all managed
to be killed in a variety of ways. Well, that makes us even. We haven't
seen any Bigfoots, but at least we're still breathing.

From a sharp rock outcrop, Patty scanned miles of valley below
with his binoculars, searching for any movement. "It's so still out
there that if a limb moves 10 miles away I'll spot it," he said.

Some believe that uninhabited wilderness no longer exists in the
Pacific Northwest—certainly not of this incredible size—but they
haven't come out here, and they never will. It's too tough. Like a
moat circling a castle, the awesome Kalmiopsis interior is surrounded by a 20-mile desolation of hot, craggy country where if the
scorpions don't get you, the lack of water and vertical trails will.
Don't bring your horse; too steep. Don't bring your dog; too little
water. Tough to get in, tough to get out. You go it alone, so you can
rely on yourself.

Unlike the high Sierra Nevada, where steep trails have
switchbacks, the trails in the Kalmiopsis wildlands practically run
straight up and straight down; there are elevation climbs of 1,500
feet in 40 minutes, followed by descents of 1,000 feet in half an
hour. You never put it in neutral. Until you reach the interior, there

is little water, just one little spring in a 12-mile span. One quart per 10 miles will have to do.

I was climbing up a rocky grade, puffing like a steam engine, when I flashed back to the training for this trip: Six months of aerobics, weightlifting, sprints and hiking Montara Mountain had dropped my resting heart rate to 59 beats per minute. When I reached the top of Grunt Ridge, my heartbeat was at 160 and thumping like a pile-driver. After a two-minute break, my body had reconciled with my mind; time to head on. That was the payback, reaching the interior in one day instead of two. Had to, that is, in order to reach water.

Man is a stranger in these woods and the animals and birds were mystified by us. Even the chipmunks kept their distance, watching, trying to figure us. In one shaded spot, I was sitting on a log, chewing on a piece of jerky, when a hummingbird dive-bombed. For an instant, he held his position just a few inches from my left ear, his wings buzzing. "Duck," shouted Jeff, and a split-second after I did so, that hummingbird shot right through the air space my head had just vacated.

"Hey man, that bird was likely to suck the juice right out of your head," Jeff said. "It didn't know what to make of you."

We were in deep, where humans rarely visit. This area is the relative size of the San Francisco Bay Area, yet instead of five million people, there were only two of us, Jeff and myself. That was it. Furniss had returned to his work as a hydrologist for the U.S. Forest Service.

I leaned back against a big cedar, chewing the last of the jerky, taking a deep breath, finally relaxing, and that peculiar sound came from the woods again.

"Thump, thump, thump, thump, thump." Five times. Like a drumstick hitting a hollow log.

"What the hell is that?" asked Patty. There was no answer. Then it stopped.

We were at Chetco Gulch, a lonely, eerie place. My thoughts

Straight up and straight down—scrambling in the Kalmiopsis wildlands

were matching the surroundings. I had this strange feeling that I was going to see Bigfoot. That night. Call it crazy if you want, call it intuition, but who knows why, the thought was there. It was the same kind of intuitive surge I sometimes feel just before I catch a trout or see a deer. That little voice in the back of my head always leads me on.

Meanwhile, in the middle of nowhere, we had found a small spring, the source for a little stream that is vital to all wildlife here. An hour before dusk, we mapped our plans. My fellow explorer, Jeff Patty, would head downstream, I would head upstream. We would find hidden perches from which to view likely spots where animals would stop to water. Dusk can be a magic time in the wilderness, when almost all creatures big and small venture to the watersheds. We split up, and after 20 minutes, I found a good overlook and began waiting, watching.

As I waited, I thought of the rare nature of the Kalmiopsis wildlands, a harsh, rugged country noted for steep trails, panoramic views and occasional Bigfoot episodes. From Canyon Peak or the crest of Fiddler Mountain, you are confronted with 360-degree panoramic views. Check it out: To the west some 30 miles away is the Pacific Ocean, with air so clear that you can actually see the white breakers of the surf. The Siskiyou Backbone in Northern California is prominent to the south, with Preston Peak jutting out above the rest of the range. Due east, 80 miles off in the horizon, a giant snow-covered peak rises above a black ridge: Mount Ashland, 7,533 feet high. And looking north, barely detectable, is a ridgeline topped by two monstrous snow-covered peaks, the Sisters Mountains near Bend, Oregon, some 160 miles away. While viewing this, I flashed back to a trip to Los Angeles, where you couldn't even see to the end of the block because of the yellow "filtered sunlight," as they call it. This was literally a world apart.

Why is it so remote up here? Because surrounding the wilderness is a vast tract of sparse, steep country where hikers can get roasted as if they were walking on a hot barbecue grill. After a few hours of looking at that red ground, it even starts to look like hot coals. So if Bigfoot does indeed patrol the Kalmiopsis interior, he does so with little interference from humans. It is an area like this where one can imagine several species of wildlife eluding the detection of man. A good example is the black-footed ferret, a wary, nocturnal weasel—now almost extinct—which has far fewer reported sightings than those of Bigfoot.

From my vantage point above the stream, I could view a prime stretch of the creek where animals would water. After 40 minutes, I had seen nothing, and although nightfall was approaching, that peculiar feeling persisted. Something was close, very close. Something big.

Suddenly, from behind me, the crack of a snapping tree branch jolted me as if I'd stuck my fingers in a light socket. My head cocked in an attempt to hear even the least discernible sound.

"Crunch-crunch." Two clear footsteps, limbs cracking beneath them, perhaps 150 feet away, hidden by the forest. Then silence. I jumped behind a huge cedar, about six feet across, to conceal myself. From behind this tree, I could hear the creature approaching. "Crunch-crunch, crunch-crunch, crunch-crunch." Twigs were snapping, leaves were crackling from the weight of the beast. It was heading straight toward me, perhaps 20 seconds from reaching my hideaway. A sensation of fear and wonder choked me. I could feel the beat of my heart in my neck. Here it comes, like a fast-burning fuse. Forty feet, 20 feet, 10 feet. For some reason, I was afraid to look. "Look!" I urged myself. "You must look!"

I jumped around the tree and saw him, face to face.

"How ya doing?" said my buddy, Jeff, whose only resemblance to Bigfoot is his size at 6-foot-5. "Hey, you're looking at me like I'm Bigfoot or something. You seen anything?"

I just stared at him, about ready to fall over in shock. Instead of waiting downriver with his camera as planned, Jeff had made a wide circle around the area, hoping to pick up wildlife tracks, and had descended from the mountain to my lookout.

I was getting spooked. Mountains can do that to you.

When we eventually returned to civilization, we walked into Little Joe's restaurant in Cave Junction, just before closing time. The place was as empty as the Kalmiopsis wildlands, and judging from the reaction to our appearance, it was a fortunate setting.

"Where have you guys been?" asked Little Joe, who of course is huge.

"The Kalmiopsis interior," Jeff replied.

"You guys went there? Nobody goes out there."

That's exactly why we went out there.

On hands and knees, you must crawl on bear trails that look like tunnels through vegetation; it is the only way to penetrate a true virgin wilderness. Only faint animal paths mark your way on the mountainous terrain, trails contoured to the ridges of steep mountain slopes. Mankind can be an unwelcome visitor in a place like this one.

If you want to see the Blue Creek wildlands in the Klamath Mountains, you have to see it like an animal. On all fours. Just to cover a mile, it took two hours to scramble down a slope, sliding down draws, creeping past thorny vines, crawling through brush.

"Footprints. Take a look," Patty said, ignoring the lightly bleeding scrapes and cuts on his arms and hands. "No claws."

We carefully inspected the footprints, set clear in the mud. Each print was about eight inches long, six inches wide, with distinct toe marks, but no claws. Patty looked at me, then grinned. "Don't get any wild ideas. We both know what it is."

The shape of the foot was the giveaway. Bigfoot's print is reputed to be more like the shape of an hourglass, not a pancake like this one. There was no doubt about it. "Bear—big one," I said.

More giant footprints reputed to be left by Bigfoot have been found here than in any place in America. And just 40 miles away at

Bluff Creek, the famous yet disputed footage of Bigfoot was filmed in 1968. The headwaters of Blue Creek is a truly secret place, almost never visited, even by the most rabid of wilderness explorers. By all accounts, it is the heart of Bigfoot Country.

"You will never see him," said Jimmy Jackson, a 75-year-old Hupa Indian and my personal adviser. "You will only see his footprints. And if you do not make peace with the mountain, you will be led to danger."

Danger? With no trails, you can get lost and never found—a slip and a sprained ankle or broken leg can leave you marooned indefinitely. Even rangers look at this area and say: "No way in, no way out. Forest is too dense to search by helicopter." The kicker is that Blue Creek is tucked away at the bottom of a 2,000-foot slope, which means a hard rain will get funneled into the creek like a sluice box—causing Blue Creek to rise from a moderate, waist-deep stream into a suicidal whitewater crossing.

Just before a descent from a steep slope into Blue Creek, Patty looked at the sun, then pointed at it. A large ring circled it. We both knew what it meant. Big rain. Big trouble.

Later, Patty slipped on a moss-covered log and banged his leg hard, his big frame going for a tumble. In minutes, his shin had a lump on it the size of a baseball. "For a minute, I thought I broke my leg," he said.

A light rain started to fall. We both felt an eerie sensation, an unexplainable sense that something strange was about to happen, and each of us mentioned it. The area was quite near what is considered a sacred ground for the Hupas, who say a "feeling of presence" is not uncommon there.

If Bigfoot was indeed a real, living creature, then it was not difficult to conceive of him living there. The Blue Creek watershed provides the habitat and quiet that Bigfoot would require. If you conform to the theory that Bigfoot is an animal, then his diet would be similar to that of a bear's—and Mr. Bear was thriving there, with droppings and footprints everywhere. There was plenty of food:

blackberries, huckleberries, edible plants and fish in the stream. As for range, on a long ridgeline there were several creeks that poured down to the main stream—and between each creek we discovered lateral trails where an animal could live and travel by contouring the slope.

Most backpackers do not even consider exploring the area. There are no trails. Blue Creek? Most people have not even heard of it. Even in the Sierra Club's outstanding guidebook, *Hiking the Bigfoot Country*, in which author John Hard describes thousands of miles of rarely-seen trails, he says this about the East Fork of Blue Creek: "I have not hiked here, and I do not know anyone who has. I do not recommend this area—except to someone who is looking for an adventure, as opposed to a hike. But if anyone finds out what is to be seen on the East Fork, I would be grateful to know."

To reach it, we traveled to the town of Orleans on Route 96, which bordered the Klamath River, then took a logging road north for 20 miles.

You talk about bears? Bears, deer, squirrels and chipmunks shadowed us. Though we sighted only a few, bear droppings and tracks were discovered almost everywhere, but especially in clearings and all along Blue Creek.

That evening, with a light rain falling, Patty rigged our packs in a makeshift pulley system in order to hang them high in a tree, out of Mr. Bear's reach. Out here, the bears see man as their only enemy and they keep their distance. Only grizzlies defend their turf and they are extinct in California because of it. The creatures that run are the ones that live. Bigfoot included.

When we descended to the stream's edge, we first found long sticks to help our stability in the water, then started to cross. "The water's a lot warmer here than in the Siskiyous," Patty shouted. But it was also deeper. It crept to our waists at midstream, rolling moderately, washing the muck from our clothes, the dried blood from the small cuts on our arms.

We spent a day traversing animal trails and hiking along the stream, crossing it several times, searching, probing the wilds for Bigfoot or his footprints. It began to drizzle, then rain. It should have been a warning. Neither of us mentioned it. The rain seemed welcome after enduring 100-degree temperatures on earlier days. But like I said, it should have been a warning.

We found out why. Twenty-eight hours later, it was still raining. Hard. The river was up, maybe as deep as my shoulders, and we were on the wrong side of it. Trying to cross it seemed like suicide.

But we were running low on food, and Patty could be as stubborn as an ox. "We're crossing," was about all he said.

I had my doubts.

It was raining so hard that if you looked up in the sky, you might almost drown. We'd seen no sign of Bigfoot and Patty wanted out. He stood at the edge of the stream, trying to assess where to attempt the crossing. "We've got to get across now, before the river rises any more," Patty said. "If we don't cross now, we might never get out of here."

At streamside, the rock I had fished from two evenings before was submerged, well under a foot of water. Since the river was waist-deep coming across, 20 inches higher now made it chin deep. It was rolling big, with crests of whitewater ramming the boulders. I wished I had gills. There were no trails in, no trails out. It wasn't the kind of place where you waited for help.

Patty, at 6-foot-5, said he could make the 60-foot crossing. "And if I can, you can," he insisted. Patty took three steps into the river, steadying himself with a tree limb, and the water quickly climbed to 10 inches above his knee. Two more steps and it was at his belt. With 45 feet to go, the river kept getting deeper and swifter.

He hesitated just for a bit. Without a word, he slowly turned around, straining against the current, working the big stick to support himself. He wobbled, and started to tip—and a second later, was going down—then he lunged toward the shoreline, but the current knocked him down. Only his head was above water, but his lunge took him to water just shallow enough where he could scramble on all fours to the bank. A close call, and a quick one, but he was safe.

Crossing was impossible. Patty, wet and chilled to the marrow, looked at the sky. Still raining. Hard. "River's still rising," he said. No way out and everything was wet; sleeping bags, clothes, firewood—and food was mighty sparse. We were getting close to the edge. We managed to build a giant campfire, tried to get warm, and talked of old Indians. After all, Hupa Indians had warned us. "The mountains there do not know you," Hupa Jimmy Jackson had told us. "Do not do anything wrong, wherever you are; otherwise the mountains will punish you."

There are many Indian legends of Bigfoot. The Yurok Indians, who live downstream on the Klamath River, call Bigfoot the "Indian Devil." Most of the Hupas, however, believe Bigfoot is a spirit; you will never see him, but find only his footprints. They also tell of the legend of Tan (pronounced "Tawn"), the immortal ruler of the woods, and Kishwish—or the Little People—two-and-a-half-foot tall creatures who live like moles in the earth.

Tan takes care of the woods and all its creatures, and is to be feared and respected, according to the Hupas. Louise Jackson, a Hupa, said that the Indians would go to the mountains and put out big bowls filled with fish and acorns as an offering. "Two weeks later, they would go back and find articles in trade in the bowls," said Minnie McWilliams, the daughter of Louise Jackson. "This was up in Blue Creek, where nobody goes."

"If you kill a deer, you leave the entrails for Tan," said Jimmy Jackson, who then reached into his pocket and extracted a root, which he said was magic. "When you hike, put medicine on your stick. There's rattlers in the brush, but the medicine on your stick is a red-tailed hawk. He's medicine because he's the one who catches the rattlers."

The Hupas believe that there are laws of the wild and they must not be violated. "They are what you call rules," Jackson said. "Don't holler. Don't throw rocks. Don't fish at more than one spot. Never carry a fish by the tail. Never throw a fish or a deer away. If you kill a rattlesnake, then kill it—don't let it suffer." If you break one of these rules, the Hupas believe the Kishwish will "take hold of you," causing you to get lost in the woods, or to become severely ill. In 1920, when Jackson was a youngster, he had such an experience.

"I tried fishing different places with my dip net, but I wasn't catching anything," Jackson said. "I got a headache, and a week later it kept on. Nobody could figure it out. Then the medicine woman came over and the old lady sang a few songs. "She told me, 'I seen you down on the river, fishing here and fishing there. What were you doing? You're not supposed to do these things. When you fish, you fish one spot. Those people in the gorge are the Little People, and they will kill you for violating the rules. I will go and ask them to let you go.' She came the next evening, sang a song before speaking. 'They said they're going to let you go,' she said. 'But never do that again. You're going to have a hollow head. They're going to take you outside, and the first thing you're going to see is a bird. Then you'll feel good.'

"The next day, my head felt like it wasn't there, and all of a sudden it was like a fire went by, a bird with every color in the rainbow. It was the bird she told me about. It was then that I felt I was myself again. It happened just like she said."

The Hupa world is a metaphysical one, and only in spirit does Bigfoot exist, according to the Indians.

Dark sky, silent thoughts. After 28 straight hours of rain, it finally lightened and stopped, but the river was raging. Our only hope was to wait it out and hope that the stream would drop to passable levels.

Patty and I each grabbed one end of my sleeping bag, then twisted it in opposite directions. As the bag corkscrewed and tightened, water squeezed out as if we were wringing out a wet rag. Our bags are filled with fiber that can retain 50 to 75 percent of your body heat even when wet. In conditions like the ones we were facing, it can keep you alive. If you're lucky, you might even go to sleep for a few minutes. A few minutes of sleep in a wet bag is quite a deal compared to permanent sleep at the bottom of a river. Patty had narrowly avoided that earlier. "We'll go again tomorrow," he vowed.

To some people, it might seem like a date with death. Crossing a stream roaring with 28 hours of storm runoff—submerged up to your chest with a 40-pound pack strapped on—is not suggested for weekend recreation. But Jeff Patty teetered his way across Blue Creek again, using an old tree limb as a wading staff. The river level had dropped eight inches and Patty had worked his way some 45 feet of the 60-foot crossing, when he stopped dead.

"A deep spot up ahead," he shouted, the river already above his waist. There was no going back, and a 40-foot waterfall waited just downriver. A slip meant riding down the suicide chute.

He crept a few more steps forward, started to teeter in the current, and I could sense he was losing it. Going down! He let out a yelp and jumped toward the shoreline, completely stretching out his 6-foot-5 frame—and the river swept him downstream some 30 feet before his knees and hands hit river bottom, his head poking above the surface. Safe. He climbed out of the water, stood on the opposite shore, and waved me on.

"Go for it," he shouted across the stream.

This is not the kind of place where you wait for help. Blue Creek has no trails for a rescue team to hike on, and the forest is so dense that a helicopter search would be useless. It was time to cross. But at 6-foot-1 instead of Patty's 6-foot-5, I was giving the river a four-inch handicap.

As I stepped in the stream, the words of Jimmy Jackson rang in my head: "If you do not make peace with the mountain, you will be led to danger."

This was the final day of the Bigfoot Expedition.

Bigfoot? The signs and hints had been many on our forays, but a little detective work revealed no evidence.

Footprints we'd discovered had turned out to be either our own boot prints melted into the snow by the warming of early summer or pancake-shaped bear tracks. A glimpse of a large hairy creature below Devil's Punchbowl? A large bear. The "crunch-crunch" walk of a two-legged creature in the Kalmiopsis wildlands did prove to be a couple of big feet, but not Bigfoot's—just my traveling compadre Jeff Patty's size 13 boots as he bushwhacked his way around camp.

The possibilities are high that many Bigfoot episodes are like these, where people with good intentions are led astray by the mysterious encounters of the wild.

"Very, very few of the people who come into our district office for wilderness permits are skilled woodsmen," said Michael Furniss. "Most of the people who are highly skilled in woodsmanship we see in the fall, and most of them are hunters. This makes it likely that many of these episodes are just mistaken. Myself, I'm skeptical."

Add in the number of hoaxes where pranksters have duped gullible tourists from outside the area, and relatively few inexplicable cases are left.

But those few remain. Like the footprints found that had dermal ridges, prints that archeologists say cannot be faked. Like the cackling shriek that is Bigfoot's cry and which cannot be duplicated without electronic equipment.

We had one inexplicable episode. It was the bizarre noise in the woods we heard in the Kalmiopsis wildlands: "Thump, thump, thump, thump, thump." Five times, like somebody hitting a hollow log with a drumstick, except there were no somebodies within 25 miles of us. It was a noise none of us had ever heard before. I kept thinking of it—that and my conversation with the old Hupa Indian.

I was waist-deep in Blue Creek, struggling just to stay upright, much less take a step, yet I was scarcely halfway across the river, with deeper water ahead. Was the old Indian's intuition right? Was the mountain out to get me? On the other side of the river, Patty was

Tom attempts the stream crossing at Blue Creek, using a tree limb for balance

waiting some 40 yards downstream, wading up to his thighs, facing me, just in case. He had already dumped, and realized my chances of doing likewise were high.

"The bad spot is just up ahead," Patty yelled.

The water was cool, fast and strong. I took each step methodically, wedging the tree limb between rocks, using it for stability to take each step. Just like a tripod, I thought. Everything seemed so quiet, all but the sound of rushing water. Then—bang! The tree limb did not catch between the rocks. It skidded off the top of one and the current knocked me down into the river, so fast it was as if I'd been hit with a shot of lightning.

My head went under water and my body started rolling downstream like a pinwheel. I thought again of Jimmy Jackson. "Make peace with the mountain." Was I now paying? Still underwater, I stabilized the rolling and looked up at the river surface, just 10 inches away. But it seemed like miles.

As the current pushed me downstream toward the waterfall, I could just barely see Patty through the water, this wild-man look branded on his face. I thrust a hand above my head and it barely cleared the surface.

Slap! Patty grabbed that single hand and we locked grips, but my tumbling weight, compounded by the force of the current, pulled him in, too. We rolled and scrambled downstream, and then suddenly, I felt the bottom of the stream on my knees. When I crawled to the bank, the roar of the waterfall sounded like a lion's roar. Safe but close. We had made it. I savored every breath.

Several hours later, we were climbing out of the Blue Creek Canyon to the four-wheel drive rig, the trip a few miles from being over. Wet, haggard, hungry and cold, I looked at Patty and sung softly, thankful to be alive.

> *Wilderness calls to him,*
> *Meadows, streams and the mountain rims.*
> *Fishing pole, deer and quail*
> *Checkin' in with the wilderness trail.*

Patty smiled and added a few more lines:
> *Animals, we've seen 'em all,*
> *But no Bigfoot can we recall.*
> *Up and down the ridge he roams*
> *He gets so wild he'll never go home.*

We rounded a bend and the truck finally came in sight. We hoisted our soggy packs into the back of the truck, and shook hands.

"A good trip," Patty said. Then he grinned. "Not so sure there's a Bigfoot out there."

Just then, that bizarre sound came from the nearby woods. "Thump, thump, thump, thump, thump." Five times. Like a drumstick hitting a hollow log. We looked at each other.

"What's out there?…"

For a map or information about the Kalmiopsis Wilderness, send $3 to Siskiyou National Forest, 200 Northeast Greenfield, P.O. Box 440, Grants Pass, OR 97526, or phone (503) 471-6500.

For a map of the Six Rivers National Forest, the Siskiyous, or Trinity Alps Wilderness, send $3 to U.S. Forest Service, 630 Sansome Street, San Francisco, CA 94111.

Tom walks through the Watershed, with San Andreas Lake in the background

AROUND THE BAY
in Seven Days

*A 126-Mile Hike from the Urban Jungle
to the Coastal Headlands*

❖

Grizzly bears bounded down the beach, huge and frightening, to tear their jaws into the flesh of the whale that had washed up in the surf. From the bluffs, tule elk and antelope watched the scene, their ears pricked for any sound, knowing that they, too, could be hunted—by wolves.

This was what the San Francisco Bay Area was like some 200 years ago, when so many whales were in the ocean and the Bay that they would spout every 30 seconds "within a pistol shot" of boats. "Countless troops" of grizzly bears roamed the land. Mountain lions, bobcat, beavers and sea otters were prominent and visible. Sea lions covered the water surface "like a pavement" in many areas. Herds of antelope and elk roamed in vast numbers, similar to the buffalo herds of the Midwestern Plains.

It was a world of little change, populated by scattered tribes of the Ohlone nation, grinding acorns and catching steelhead, and always fearing an unexpected meeting with a big griz. Imagine that! This is the way the Bay Area was found by explorers in the early 1800s, according to their diaries. Here are excerpts unearthed by author Malcolm Margolin in *The Ohlone Way:*

"*There is not any country in the world which more abounds in fish and game of every description. (Geese and ducks rise) in a dense cloud with a noise like that of a hurricane. (The land has) inexpressible fertility.*"—Jean La Perouse, French sea captain

"*Animals seem to have lost their fear and become familiar with man…(Quail) are so tame that they would often not start from a stone directed at them. (Rabbits) can sometimes be caught with the hand.*"—Captain Frederick Beechy

"*Geese, ducks and snipes were so tame that we might have killed great numbers with our sticks…Never have seen game in such abundance…there is a superfluity of game.*"—Russian explorer Otto von Kotebue

"*(Grizzly bears) are horrible, fierce, large and fat. Several Indians are badly scarred by the bites and scratches of these animals.*"—Father Pedro Font

Today there are no grizzlies in the San Francisco Bay Area, of course. The only one left in California is on the state flag. No wolves are left, either. In the past 200 years, the Bay Area has gone through some of the fastest and most marked changes of any area in the world. That is why I decided to try to walk around the Bay, about 125 miles in all, from mountain tops to marshy tidelands, from mean city streets to country estates. I wanted to get a close-up view of the Bay Area and compare it to the world described in those old diaries by the area's first explorers. I knew that the present-day Bay Area is a land those first explorers would never recognize.

I planned to walk 15 to 25 miles per day, completing the trip in a week. My route would start at the south end of the Golden Gate Bridge on the San Francisco headlands, then venture south along the Peninsula, across the Dumbarton Bridge and up to the East Bay ridgeline. From there, I would hike north to the hills above Richmond, then drop down and head west across the Richmond-San Rafael Bridge and south through Marin County, finally crossing the

Golden Gate Bridge. The ultimate loop hike.

The unknowns gave the trip an edge, an element of danger. The planned route would take me through a few violent, drug-gutted neighborhoods, where a long-bearded man with a pack and a canteen appears about as often as a polar bear in the desert. But far from the street demons would await some of the most spectacular settings in America: two-thousand-foot peaks with extraordinary lookouts over San Francisco, miles of untouched shoreline along both ocean and bay, and wildlands where deer, coyote and mountain lion are residents and mankind is still a visitor.

The Bay Area has 65 lakes and 125 parks, and locals have shown a strong desire to secure more open space and parks. With 5.5

million residents and the population still growing, the Bay Area will likely need them. So many people in a relatively small amount of space can make for conflict.

That was obvious to me as I stood at the southeastern end of the Golden Gate Bridge, preparing to take the first steps of the journey around the Bay. The scene looked like paint-by-numbers artwork: A few puffy Ansel Adams clouds hovered over the Bay, and early-morning sunlight and light breezes sent metallic slivers across the water. A tugboat cruised under the bridge against the background of Belvedere, Angel Island and Alcatraz.

But just a few dozen yards away, at the southern access to the Golden Gate Bridge, traffic was gumming up like settling concrete. For commuters, the Bay's beauty can be of little matter, and you see that in their tight, squinted eyes as they drive. Considering what they are going through, it's hard to blame them.

From the Golden Gate, the 9.1-mile Coastal Trail heads west out to Land's End, where city meets ocean. You walk along a dirt trail sprinkled with pine needles, near bluffs topped with cypress trees. An assortment of poppies, blooming ice plant and wild grasses decorate the path. The views are among the best in the Bay Area: You see the mouth of the Bay, crashing breakers in the foreground, the Farallon Islands and Point Reyes out along the horizon to the west. From a bluff, looking out to the ocean a few miles, I saw what looked like a puff of smoke shooting up, a whale spout. Some 200 years ago, whales were a common sight spouting near the mouth of the Bay. While I stood there hoping to see the spout again, some brown pelicans, an endangered species, glided past. They are reminders of the many special creatures that still live here, and of those that once did, but no longer do.

A few minutes later, I rounded a bend. A big rock had been spray painted with the words, "Commune with nature—die."

As you hike, you can't help but sense the contrast between the old and the new world. After rounding the Cliff House at Land's End and heading south along Ocean Beach, that contrast was vividly displayed to me. Out to sea, an old wooden sailboat bobbed in the swells. Nothing else was around. It was slowly moving south, melding into the scenery, quiet and alone. But ashore, a short distance from that old boat, a homeless person was looking through a garbage can, people were dropping their litter and burning cigarettes on the ground, and teenagers were sitting on the hoods of their cars drinking beer, the doors wide open, rap music blasting.

The first day's hike was routed past Land's End, south past Ocean Beach and Lake Merced, and onward along Skyline Boulevard to Skyline College, about 17 miles. Because there were no camping areas along my route, a shuttle system was necessary each day. Each morning, I left my truck at the day's destination, then was shuttled back to the starting point.

Off in the distance, Montara Mountain loomed solitary at 2,000 feet, like an old sentinel, unchanged for thousands of years, watching the changes below.

I took the San Francisco Peninsula as my destination for the trip's second leg. Out there you'll find a piece of land that remains much the same as when the first Europeans to come West found it 200 years ago. It starts at Sweeney Ridge above San Bruno, the Bay's discovery site, and sprawls south for 15 miles, a natural paradise where deer, mountain lions and wild trout are welcome—and people are not.

Insiders simply call it the "Watershed," since it is land owned by the San Francisco Water Department. But no other metropolitan area in the world has a piece of turf like this. It covers 23,000 acres, contains four lakes and three streams, is cut by an active earthquake fault line and is bordered by 2,000-foot peaks on one side and huge meadows on the other where deer browse by the dozen. In my route around the Bay I had a rare chance to explore this area, provided after I obtained a special permit for access. The bottom line is that it is an official state Fish and Game Refuge, an area set aside to protect wildlife and fish.

From the ridgetop, you can see many miles in all directions, and a striking contrast is before you: millions of residents connected in a chain of suburbia on the flatlands, but bordered by the expansive waters of the South Bay on one side, and the wide-open spaces of the foothill country on the other. There is no middle ground.

You walk into the refuge, and you scarcely feel you are in the Bay Area. At one point, my companion Jim McDaniel and I stopped to rest at a meadow bordering San Andreas Lake. It was a remarkable scene: Deer were silhouetted on the hill behind us, trout were jumping in the lake, and mushrooms the size of dinner plates were growing in the meadow, along with flowering poppies, wild irises and lupine. Everything seemed unique, even the trees. At the north end of San Andreas Lake we found a giant cypress tree 40 feet long and 8 feet wide, with multiple trunks—11 different trees growing out of the same trunk.

"This could be the Yukon Territory for all I know," McDaniel said. "It's hard to believe this place exists just a few minutes from Highway 280."

Every step in the Watershed seems special. We started this day's trip on the trailhead at Skyline College, a nice break after walking on pavement for the previous 12 miles. It's just a 40-minute walk up to Sweeney Ridge, where explorer Gaspar de Portola first viewed San Francisco Bay, and they say his neck still hurts. It's easy to see why, because you need a 360-degree swivel to see everything. There is no better place for a panorama of the South Bay. But you push on, because you're eager to explore the rest of the wildlands. In four hours, we counted 30 deer, along with many squirrels, rabbits and jumping trout. And you learn quickly why the bush bunnies jump around so fast here—hawks circle above, looking for lunch.

It was mid-morning as we hiked along the shore of northern Crystal Springs Lake. The sky looked like a bed mattress, a high wall of clouds edged by little puffs of white. We stopped where a stream was feeding into the northern shallows of Crystal Springs and watched the trout jump, one after another. I felt a familiar yearning well up inside me—to try and catch a few.

You can sit and watch them jump all day, but that is all you're allowed to do. This is the only fish refuge in the nation. Alas, people try anyway. Two friends of mine did just that, and in 15 minutes caught three 20-inch rainbow trout. Five minutes later, they had been handcuffed and were taking a trip to the county jail. Their fine for poaching in a fish refuge was three nights in jail and $750 apiece, $250 per trout. About 50 people per month are arrested trying to sneak into the refuge, according to Water Department figures. Hiking permits are rarely provided to organized groups, but fishing is never permitted and the area is always heavily patrolled.

"Look, but don't touch," is the message, and never forget it.

To accommodate lookers, a good public trail runs along the eastern side of the Watershed. The best of it is called the Sawyer Camp Trail, a paved pathway that tunnels through heavy vegetation and a dense forest of mixed hardwoods. It seems a place of perfect peace until a maniacal bike rider explodes around a blind corner and rips your whiskers off at 30 miles per hour.

There's another element of the Sawyer Camp Trail that can literally give you the jitters: It's the zone for the San Andreas Fault, that is, earthquake country. The trail crosses the fault twice, and you can see how the plants and wildlife grow differently on either side.

"Right now we are up to 13 feet of strain on the fault," said Steven Durkin, a county ranger I met while hiking here. "When the '06 earthquake occurred, it released eight feet of displacement on the Sawyer Camp Trail."

Well, as far as my companion McDaniel was concerned, there was an earthquake in his hiking boots every time he took a step. His boots were a bit small, his feet had swelled up, and the combination was causing him to jam his toes into the ends of his boots with every step.

"I know this is a game refuge, but I didn't know they had alligators," he said. "It feels like a couple have snuck into my boots and are biting my feet."

My feet felt kind of like I was walking barefoot on ice picks. The signs along the watershed say, "Loitering is forbidden by law," and at the speed we were going, I'm surprised we didn't get arrested. We crossed Highway 92 and McDaniel even hobbled up to an old guy who was parked, reading a newspaper, and tried to bribe him to take him home. The guy just rolled the window up. Keep walking, Jim. Well, he did, about 20 miles in all, and all it cost him were 10 black-and-blue toenails, five of which he lost the next week.

After hiking through the Peninsula foothills, I crossed through Woodside, then headed west through Stanford and Menlo Park and East Palo Alto and across the Dumbarton Bridge. On the Newark side of the bridge is a unique marshland that is a National Wildlife Refuge and parkland.

To get there, you must first cross through Woodside, the Beverly Hills of the Bay Area. "Are you the guy who is supposed to rake the leaves?" asked a woman standing next to a gated driveway, the wrought iron tipped with brass spires. I looked behind me to see who she was addressing, but there was nobody there.

In Woodside, you are more likely to see somebody on a horse than on foot. This is money country and you see it in every move. Some of the people even seem to adopt strange styles of walking, maybe to make sure you know they aren't "just anybody." You know, they can't be walking around like you or me. As for me, I think I'll just mosey along. No thanks, I stopped raking leaves when I was a teenager.

The Peninsula's Woodside region is also rich in natural beauty, with rolling hills, old trees and young wildflowers. In the meadows, it is common to see deer and rabbits, with big flocks of meadow-larks swooping about, especially in the spring.

Walking from Woodside to East Palo Alto in a few hours provides one of the sharpest contrasts in lifestyle in the Bay Area. After seeing bright patches of wildflowers in a woodside meadow, it was a shock to the senses to see fresh, bright red blood on the pavement next to an East Palo Alto bus stop. But there it was, still wet.

A few people were waiting, oblivious to it.

"What happened?" I asked one fellow.

"Hey man, you don't want to know," he said.

I kept walking. A hundred yards farther away, beside a fence in broad daylight, two young guys and a girl were trading brown paper bags. While I described the scene into my pocket tape recorder, all three suddenly sprinted away, as if I were an undercover agent. Well, undercover agents don't usually wear a pack and a canteen.

The blood on the pavement at that bus stop made me feel like a soldier on a march. I didn't feel like sitting on a rock and gazing at the urban scene, even if there were any rocks for sitting. In a half hour, I was leaving town, nearing the South Bay's marshlands and the entrance ramp to the Dumbarton Bridge.

When I reached the expanse of water and marshlands at the Bay's edge, I felt free and alone, just me and the critters of the tidelands. The craziness, anger and violence was just a mile away, but already it seemed a fresh new world.

The Dumbarton Bridge has a biking and hiking path that is separated from traffic by a cement cordon. I marched on, then stopped at a perch at the bridge's highest point, at center span. The reward is one of the greatest views of the Bay Area and its surrounding ridgelines. On a clear day, it looks like you can reach out and touch all the major peaks: Mount Hamilton, Mount Diablo, Mount Tamalpais, Montara Mountain and Sweeney Ridge. You are encircled by water and the South Bay's tidal marshlands. Some 200 years ago, the Bay Area flatlands were swamp-like, with vast marshes of cordgrass and tules supporting millions of ducks, wildlife and fish. Today the creeks have been channeled, the pumping of groundwater has lowered the water table, and more than 50 percent of the Bay's marshes have been lost to landfill. But they ain't got 'em all. At the southeast end of the Dumbarton Bridge is the 23,000-acre San Francisco Bay Wildlife Refuge that still acts as one of the major rest stops for millions of migratory birds of the Pacific Flyway. I continued walking toward this special habitat.

A diversity of critters inhabit the shores of the Bay here, from tiny crabs to herons. They have lived here practically since the beginning of time. A double handful of mud can contain 40,000 tiny creatures, the primary level of the marine food chain.

The Wildlife Refuge is a special place, where nature's cycles still phase in and out with regard to seasons—and without regard to mankind. In the areas around the Bay that are still largely un-touched, wildlife can thrive. In other areas, it simply cannot.

The stretch from Newark to Hayward is one dry piece of life. It's a hot, flat mass of concrete, and wherever you find a field of wild-flowers you can bet there's someone plotting to pave it over in the next five years.

But just a few miles away, hidden in the canyons of the open foothill country, are more than a dozen lakes. On blue-sky days, they can look like jewels sparkling in the sun.

It is like this around much of the Bay Area. You can find a ribbon of concrete on the flatlands, yet parks and hidden lakes in the hills. Most people know about the former but have only a hint about the latter. There are 65 lakes in the Bay Area foothills, but most people have trouble naming more than three or four. Although virtually all were built in case of a public water shortage, the lakes also provide a relatively new support system for fish, birds and wildlife.

In the early 1800s, the Bay Area's plentiful wildlife did not need any reservoirs. It's one of the drastic changes in the Bay Area since the area was first visited, then settled, by outsiders. The change came early in the nineteenth century with the arrival of the rifle.

There were no game laws then; in fact, what was called the "State Division of Fish and Game" was not established until more than 100 years later, in 1927. In the meantime, locals made their own laws, and in the process, grizzlies were shot to extinction, and elk and antelope were annihilated. Beavers and otters were virtually eliminated by trapping, and anything that flew was a target. Most of the remaining wildlife was then pushed out by encroachment from pioneer settlers.

In the past 50 years, loss of wildlife habitat has further decimated fish and animal populations. Over 50 percent of the Bay has been filled, all but a scant percentage of wetlands have been lost to fill and pavement, and most of the streams have been channeled by concrete, polluted and left unfit for life.

The animals, fish and birds remaining are relatively secretive, many nocturnal, even though hunting has virtually ceased as a sport in the Bay Area. What is left are moats of wildlife habitat around the 65 man-made reservoirs and 125 parklands in the Bay Area foothills.

One man who has seen much of the change is Harold Patton of Oakland. While hiking a steep, remote piece of trail set in dense cover in Huckleberry Regional Park, I spotted him creeping around, laying dog food near the bases of trees.

"I'm feeding the foxes," he said. "They will eat just about anything, you know. They live on mice now, little mice. I've watched them catch them. I've been coming up here since 1924, when I was just a boy."

Then he paused and looked across the slope of the mountain.

"Up at the top there's an eagle nest, and last year, the eagle laid an egg. It happened on February 27 and they flew away on the first of June. You could see them.

"I'm kind of like a general patrol. When I first came here there were thousands of quail all around, and ground squirrels. They poisoned off the ground squirrels in 1936. Ground squirrels! Someone had the idea that they had poison fleas and carried bacteria. Ever since then, there aren't as many foxes, you know, or hawks either, because they would live off the squirrels."

At many habitats around the Bay Area, sometimes the best wildlife management is to do nothing. Yet time and time again, mankind has inflicted pain on the land under the mistaken pretense that it was all for the best.

Eighty miles into my hike, I passed through Hayward and into Chabot Regional Park in the foothills above Castro Valley, where I found a gem of a spot. If you yearn to get away from city life for a while, Chabot's Grass Valley can provide a simple, easy-to-reach paradise.

Hayward is a wicked place to go for a walk, with nothing but concrete and cars for miles. Except for adding a tattoo parlor, it hasn't improved much in the past 200 years. Of course, neither have a lot of places. But it takes just a few steps on the dirt trail of Chabot Regional Park—finally, off pavement—and the world seems to be in tune again, especially in Grass Valley.

In the backcountry of the East Bay hills, this meadow lines a valley floor for more than a mile, framed by the rims of miniature mountains on each side. In the spring, it's bright green and loaded with blooming wild radish, blue-eyed grass and golden poppies. It's quiet and beautiful; nothing extra is needed.

I planned to hike the East Bay Skyline Trail, which starts at the southern end of Chabot Park and runs 31 miles to Wildcat Canyon Regional Park in the hills above Richmond. The trail generally follows the ridgeline, linking six parks, and although it's only a short distance from civilization on the flats below, you can feel quite distant and remote on many sections of this trail.

Sometimes on long expeditions, I'll just stop in places like this, have a seat and consider how perfect everything can seem in a wild setting. I was doing just this in Grass Valley when I felt something crawling on my arm. "Well hello there, little ant." Innocently, I looked down and saw swarms of them on my hiking boots, and more climbing up on my jeans. I had sat on a colony and was being declared a National Ant Sanctuary. I squished all the little buggers I could find, but for the next few hours, I itched like crazy, imagining little crawlies creeping all over me.

The Ohlone, the original dwellers of the Bay Area, probably had problems like that, too. Along with grizzly bears occasionally biting them. Some say the ghosts of the Ohlone still watch over these hills. You can still sense the presence of the old Indians in wild areas, even though the ways of the Ohlone have been all but snuffed out in modern Bay Area life. If the Indians of two centuries ago were to return today, they would find the views unbelievable.

From the East Bay ridgeline looking west, the refracted sunlight of late afternoon makes San Francisco look like an Emerald City. With the sun behind it, the Golden Gate Bridge sparkles, even from 15 miles away. Giant cargo ships, tankers and sailboats bring the Bay alive. And so many cars, thousands of them, make the highways look like veins in a pulsing heart.

How would the Ohlone react to such a sight? Probably the same way I did in Grass Valley—be glad you're seeing it from a distance, then hit the trail and search for a place of more solitude.

That isn't hard in the East Bay Regional Park District. The Skyline Trail climbs a ridge heading north, crosses Redwood Road, then connects to Redwood Regional Park. There, a network of trails are routed north six miles, where they link up with another park, Huckleberry Preserve. The chance for adventure is unlimited.

No matter which way you go, what you find is a surprise. Redwood trees—that's right, in the East Bay hills, a thick forest of them. They line canyon walls for miles in Redwood Regional Park, enclosing a small, beautiful trout stream at its center. The fish here provide one of the few direct links to an earlier time, a pure strain of native trout, descendants from a time when Ohlone shared the land with fish and wildlife—and Hayward did not yet exist.

❖ ❖ ❖ ❖

From the trailhead at Wildcat Canyon Park in the Richmond hills, it is a two-mile hike with an 800-foot elevation gain to San Pablo Ridge. You can also reach the ridge from the south, starting at Inspiration Point in Tilden Regional Park, then hike north about five miles, most of it downhill. Either way you go, you get a view of the Bay Area that can change how you feel about this area.

To the east are San Pablo and Briones reservoirs—big, beautiful lakes; from the ridge they look like sapphires. To the north, far off in Napa Valley, is Mount St. Helena, best seen in the morning when the air is clearest. To the southeast is Mount Diablo, the bald old mountain that Ohlone Indians believed was the sacred birthplace of the world. And to the west, of course, is San Francisco Bay and the city, the Golden Gate and the open waters of the Bay. From this lookout, the islands in the Bay look like gold nuggets—Angel Island, Alcatraz and Treasure Island are the famous ones.

In just a few hours of walking, you can venture from the Bay Area's most remote and spectacular lookout points on San Pablo Ridge on the East Bay Skyline Trail, to the bleak streets of west Richmond. My route took me right through Richmond as I headed west for Marin County.

"Lower Cutting (Avenue) and thereabouts is not too good a place to be," said a Richmond cop, who helped plan the hiking route through town. "There are some problems."

I crossed the path of some kids, each perhaps about 10 years old and 65 pounds. One had a hammer in his hand and he was beating on everything he passed: trees, light posts, mailboxes. The other would occasionally give the offending object a good kick. I just kept walking, never looking back, only forward. There was plenty to look at ahead, anyway. As you go, you find graffiti everywhere: "We don't need a war on drugs, we need a war on the system." Somebody went to a lot of work to write that one, spray painted in letters 10 feet tall, high on the wall of an old fire-gutted building. Then there was a fancy one, written in script on buildings all over the city: "Unleash the fury of women as a mighty force of revolution."

What was actually being unleashed was the fury of a spray paint can. Telephone poles, sidewalks, mailboxes, old cars and old buildings—anything was fair game. Down by "the tracks," as they call the railroad freight line here, there was a switch box that had been blasted with greens, blacks and reds all over it—no words, just lines, Xs and squiggles.

The area seemed tough, with heat rising from the railroad tracks, an oil-stained road, houses with broken windows and spray-painted concrete. I suddenly stopped my hike, turned and looked back across the land I had crossed. The smog made the East Bay skyline a bit hazy in the distance, as if you couldn't see it clearly from here because it is such a different world from that of the cold, urban streets.

When I rounded Yellow Bluff on the Marin County shoreline and spotted the Golden Gate Bridge…well, after walking 120 miles, it felt like coming home. San Francisco waited just across the Golden Gate, like the land of Oz. This is where the trip started, at the southeast corner of the Golden Gate Bridge, where I began walking south for a modern-day expedition around the San Francisco Bay.

In 1789, the Bay Area was settled by Ohlone Indians, about 10,000 in all, sprinkled in different tribes from Point Sur to the North Bay. They patterned their lives after the rhythms of the oak tree. The acorn harvest marked the beginning of a new year, winter was marked by so many full moons after the harvest, and summer by so many full moons before the next harvest.

Today, in a relatively recent phenomenon, the rhythm by which people live is determined primarily by the traffic pattern of the daily commute. Two hundred years ago, a good acorn crop on the towering valley oaks in the valleys and black oaks in the hills was met with joy and festivals. Today, being able to drive 20 miles without having an accident slow you up is cause for a similar celebration.

At Corte Madera, en route from San Rafael on the last day of the trip, I crossed a footbridge over Highway 101. Below was the "freeway," which was jammed at a standstill. Even though my body felt like rigor mortis was setting in from the number of miles I had hiked, I had rarely felt so happy to be walking instead of driving.

My route took me inland along the slopes of Mt. Tamalpais, then south toward San Francisco. A superb biking/jogging/hiking path runs from San Quentin Prison near San Rafael through Corte Madera, Sausalito and Fort Baker to the northern foot of the Golden Gate Bridge. It is linked by town streets only a few times.

One stretch of this route passed through the Bothin Marsh Open Space Preserve, bordering Richardson Bay. As I passed, it was a low tide, and hundreds of little sandpipers were poking around in the mud. In a nearby slough, not much more than a small tidal waterway bordered by pickleweed, a night heron, egret and pelican were floating around together, holding a conference. That was a rare sight, and part of what still makes the Bay Area a special place.

There are still niches left where wildlife can be found and places where anyone can find peace and solitude. What a week! From untouched shorelines to 2,000-foot ridgelines, from foothill wildlands to raw city streets.

I climbed the grade from Fort Baker to Vista Point, then headed straight for the bridge. It wasn't long till I was over water, walking out the last miles of the trip.

Suddenly I stopped, leaned against the railing at the center of the Golden Gate Bridge and gazed across San Francisco Bay, looking from the East Bay Ridge to San Francisco, remembering the paths I had crossed. Even though I have lived in the area most of my life, having walked through and around it made it seem like a new world, both good and bad. For a moment, I just stared out across the Bay and felt an upwelling of feeling for my homeland. It was like a strong rain after a dust storm. Then I moved on to finish the hike.

As I crossed the Golden Gate Bridge, it felt ironic that there was no one to greet me as I closed out the last steps on this long trip. Shouldn't there be at least one person to greet me? It didn't look like it.

But as I neared the end of the bridge, there suddenly appeared several men with video cameras.

"What television station are you from?" I asked one of the camera men.

He responded in Japanese, which was completely unintelligible to me. I turned and looked behind me—and there was his vacationing family waving at the camera. They were just tourists out to see the Golden Gate Bridge.

Heh, heh, heh. It was another lesson that when it comes to the outdoors, publicity and notoriety are irrelevant. The only important elements are the experiences and feelings you have on the trail.

The Bay Area has a lot of bests and worsts. While walking the final miles of this trip, I made a list of my winners:

•*Town with the most smiles:* Woodside. Nice folks here, all of them smiling as they head to the local Wells Fargo.
•*Town with the least smiles:* Hayward. Maybe it's all the concrete.
•*Best lookouts:* San Pablo Ridge (Wildcat Regional Park), Sweeney Ridge (Golden Gate National Recreation Area), Coastal Trail (Golden Gate National Recreation Area) on the San Francisco headlands.
•*Worst gift shop:* San Quentin Prison. I couldn't even find a spoon to find for Mom's collection.
•*Most indecipherable graffiti:* West Richmond. Xs, lines squiggles.
•*Most considerate bike riders:* Tilden Park, East Bay Regional Park

District, Inspiration Point on north. They not only slow down for you, but even smile.

•*Least considerate bike riders:* Sawyer Camp Trail, Redwood City. Self-absorbed pedalers rip by without regard to anyone.

•*Ranger of the year:* Jim Silliman, Chabot Regional Park. In the middle of a hot, 20-miler of a day, and running low on water, I ran into Jim by accident—and he filled up my canteen with water from his.

•*Designer clothes award:* Sausalito. Alas, they haven't figured out that doing good beats looking good.

•*Pseudo-intellectual award:* Ocean Beach, San Francisco. This is where life's philosophy suddenly becomes clear to those looking down the barrels of beer bottles.

•*Place most in need of a rock:* Newark to Hayward. Hey, a hiker needs a place to sit now and then; in 10 miles here, there is not even a single spot.

•*Prettiest walk:* From Grass Valley to Bort Meadow in Chabot Regional Park, a lush meadow in full bloom.

•*Best sight:* The Golden Gate Bridge, viewed from Yellow Bluff at Fort Baker in Marin. After walking 10 hours per day for a week, the end of the trip was finally in sight. Nothing else even came close to beating that one.

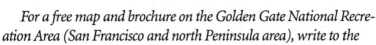

For a free map and brochure on the Golden Gate National Recreation Area (San Francisco and north Peninsula area), write to the National Park Service, Building 201, Fort Mason, San Francisco, CA 94123, or phone (415) 556-0560.

For information on the San Francisco Bay National Wildlife Refuge, write to P.O. Box 524, Newark, CA 94560, or phone (510) 792-0222.

For information on the East Bay Regional Park District, write to 11500 Skyline Boulevard, Oakland, CA 94619, or phone (510) 635-0135 ext. 2200. Free maps and brochures are available.

For information on the Marin headlands, write to the Golden Gate National Recreation Area, Building 1056, Fort Cronkite, Sausalito, CA 94965, or phone (415) 331-1540.

For information on the paved access trails around the Watershed (Sawyer Camp Trail and San Andreas Trail), write to the San Mateo County Parks and Recreation Department, County Government Center, 590 Hamilton Street, Redwood City, CA 94063, or phone (415) 363-4020. There is no other public access to the Watershed.

Tom weighs in a halibut that bottoms out the scale

OF BIG FISH
and
GRIZZLIES

Travels in the Alaskan Wildlands

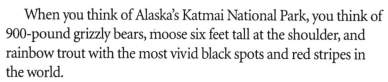

When you think of Alaska's Katmai National Park, you think of 900-pound grizzly bears, moose six feet tall at the shoulder, and rainbow trout with the most vivid black spots and red stripes in the world.

The wilderness spans some 4.2 million acres of soft tundra, surrounded by mountains cut by glaciers and mushroomed by volcanoes. There are hundreds of lakes and streams here, providing the setting for Alaska's best trout fishing. Mankind is still just a visitor at Katmai, but the wilderness and its resident fish and wildlife attract people from all over the world in summer.

Katmai is located in southwest Alaska, about 300 miles from Anchorage, where people travel by float planes, not cars. It takes a lifetime to dream about coming here, but only one day to do it. A jet flight to Anchorage, a float-plane ride to the bush country, and by 6 p.m. I was waist deep in the Kulik River, fly casting for big rainbows—my first visit to the Alaska wilderness.

The water was so clear that I could see whitefish dodging my footsteps. I whipped my fly rod back and forth twice, then let the line sail softly toward a grassy bank, the wooly worm fly settling on the surface, then sinking slowly and beginning to drift downstream.

Twitch-twitch—I felt a light nibble on the fly. With my left hand, I twitched the line right back—and wham! A trout rammed it and grabbed it. The trout jumped three times, sprinted for faster water, then dove, bulldogged and jumped again. By the time I had it alongside me, I had figured it for a trophy.

"How big?" shouted guide Wayne Hansen from shore, keeping a lookout for bears.

It looked about 18 inches, and it glistened in the evening sun as the river ran past it. Hansen just smiled as I released it.

"That's just a little one," he said. "In the next week, you'll see bigger fish than you've ever imagined."

Imagine not only rainbow trout, but big Mackinaws and scads of grayling, along with runs of king, sockeye and silver salmon—so many sockeyes in some rivers that the water is colored red by them.

Kulik Lodge, our base of operations for this trip, is positioned perfectly for a wilderness fishing expedition. It is one of three lodges in Katmai National Park which provide cabins, food, tackle and fly-out trips. In September, when trout fishing peaks, the average rainbow trout on the Kulik River is a five-pounder. I saw a 38-incher. Imagine that: A 38-inch rainbow trout! But this is Alaska, and everything seems to come big up here. The records for Kulik Lodge include a 20-pound rainbow trout, a 22-pound silver salmon, a 32-pound Mackinaw trout and a five-and-a-quarter-pound grayling, all caught on fly rods.

The Katmai is so vast that the bulk of it eludes most travelers. But even short visits, perhaps touring different areas by float plane, can provide a sample of this raw country and a sense of the natural forces that created it.

The mountain range is one of the few where both glaciers and volcanoes are at work. Glaciers have gouged out canyons and valleys, many of which have been filled with long, narrow lakes. The jagged mountain ridges look as if they were carved by a giant sculptor. Dozens of other peaks, however, are near-symmetrical volcanic cones, with 15 still active. Steam flumes still rise from

Mount Mageik, Mount Martin, Mount Triden, and of course, Mount Redoubt, the most recent volcano to blow its top, which continues to pump a white steam cloud. They are unpredictable and huge, like so much of the wildlife here.

The critters that call the Katmai home can be on the ornery side. They include the big grizzlies, Alaskan brown bears, and mosquitoes, which you learn to fear every bit as much as the big bears. It is common to see huge moose hoofprints along stream banks, and not unusual to see the prints of wolves. You are apt to run across porcupines, ground squirrels and more bald eagles than you've ever seen in your life.

One warm evening, I waded into the Kulik, made a cast and got a strange feeling that "something" was watching me. Innocently, I turned my head and looked over my shoulder. Well, that "something" turned out to be a nine- or 10-foot grizzly, just sitting in the grass along the stream watching me, maybe waiting for me to hook a fish. It looked like a Volkswagen with hair.

As soon as our eyes met, he hopped in the river and began swimming toward me. For a moment, I froze, somewhat in shock, then started moving downriver.

"You want my spot," I said, "Okay, okay. You get my spot."

While I headed downstream, the bear stopped to play a bit in the river right where I had been casting. A few minutes later, he crossed the stream and went on his way. I went back to look at his footprints in a sandbar, and they were 11 inches long, two inches deep. You learn quickly to defer to bears, clearing out whenever one arrives. It doesn't take much convincing. You can take the biggest and meanest guys you know to the Katmai, from Hells Angels to NFL linebackers, put them face-to-face with a grizzly, and they suddenly experience an "attitude adjustment."

Believe it or not, a similar mental process occurs when you see a swarm of mosquitoes moving in toward you. They make a hum that sounds like a squadron of high-powered electric fans. You can thank God and science that the mosquitoes here haven't built up an immunity to bug juice. One reason the mosquitoes are so abundant is the length of summer days. The sun typically rises at about 3:30 a.m., then sets at midnight. So the mosquitoes have 20 hours a day to hatch, build up an appetite, then set out in search for blood.

The long hours of daylight also encourage the ambitious angler, who can fish 15 to 20 hours a day. Because it takes so long for the sun to set, moving horizontally across the sky rather than vertically, the evening trout rise can last six or seven hours.

Another element that makes the Katmai special is that the primary rivers are actually short links between lakes. That means that bad weather, which can turn so many expensive Alaskan vacations into losers by turning green water into brown, is not a factor in the Katmai.

"It could rain for 40 days and 40 nights. Noah might have to build an ark, but anybody can still catch trout on the Kulik River," said Sonny Petersen, manager of the lodge. "The Kulik River has never been washed out in 40 years."

All of the fishing here is with fly rods, and all of the fish must be released. In the 1940s, when trout predation of salmon eggs was mistakenly thought to damage the commercial salmon fishery, a five-cent bounty on the tails of rainbow trout was established. It's since gone fully the other direction. In the '90s, the wild trout here are considered too valuable to be caught only once. But there are so many of them, you don't need much experience to get hookups. The standard gear is a No. 6/7 fly rod, a sinking line, six-pound test leader, and wooly bugger patterns in many colors, though black is best. In a week, I caught 175 to 200 fish, too many to keep track of, including 50 to 60 rainbow trout on the final day, which was drizzly and overcast—the best weather for fishing here. The biggest fish included a 10-pound sockeye salmon, an eight-pound Mackinaw and an 18-inch grayling.

But it was at a small stream called Petersen Creek, named after one of Alaska's legendary float-plane aviators, Ray Petersen, where magic unfolded on a warm Alaskan afternoon. This winding stream was just 10 to 20 yards wide, shallow enough to wade across. But every 50 or 60 yards, the river would offer deep holes that looked perfect to hold giant rainbow trout, the kind that account for why people come from all over the world to fish in Alaska.

I knew a giant fish was here, and while I attempted to hook him, I started calling him "Luther." But by mid-afternoon, Luther was still eluding me. In the process of trying for him, I had caught fish after fish, some 25 grayling and a dozen trout. In one 40-yard stretch, I had hookups on 14 straight casts.

Then I rounded a bend, and spotted a deep riffle that poured into a water hole, at least 15 feet deep, set at a left curve in the stream. I looked closer. A mayfly hatch was just starting, and then suddenly, a huge trout took one off the surface for a meal, leaving a two-foot whirlpool.

It looked like Luther. I looked over my shoulder for company. No bears, no guide. Just Luther and me, out in the Alaskan wilderness.

I switched to a floating line and a dry fly, and approaching from the side, cast across the head of the riffle. The fly landed softly on the surface, then drifted along the edge of the bank, next to a log, then around it. I noticed I was holding my breath. Just then, a big trout appeared from that deep blue hole of Alaskan stream. With a swirl, it grabbed the fly and disappeared. I set the hook and it was like I'd jabbed that trout with a cattle prod. The trout immediately jumped, and even from a distance, its bright red stripe was glistening. It jumped four more times in the first two minutes, ripping line in 10-yard bursts, then burrowed to the bottom of the hole. I just held on for the ride, cannons going off in my chest.

The trout came up again, cutting across the fast water, then reversing field and running straight downstream. It sprinted 30 yards before I was able to turn it, my rod bowed and bouncing. For 10 minutes, it was give and take, the trout leading me a quarter-mile downstream. After several more shorter bursts, I led the fish across an eddy to a gravel bar.

It was Luther all right, 25 inches long, seven or eight inches across, with a brightness and beauty that no picture or painting could capture. I unhooked the fly from his lip, set him in a few feet of water, and in a flash he was gone, back to his home in the water hole.

Instead of making another cast, I just sat on a rock for awhile, watching the water go by, looking at the mountains in the distance. This is the true Alaska, the great frontier that still offers visitors a chance at their dreams.

People are fascinated by grizzly bears because every once in a while one will decide to take a bite out of somebody's head.

That and other similar thoughts ran through my mind as we looked down at a big footprint left in the soft sand along the river. Nearby, the carcass of a sockeye salmon was lying perfectly intact, except for a giant hole where its heart should have been.

Suddenly, our .44 caliber handgun, which once seemed big enough to put a hole in the moon, didn't seem so big anymore.

I was hired by a lodge to team up with a seasonal guide to search out new fishing areas that they could offer to new clients. This was at the headwaters of the Talachulitna River, near Judd Lake, about 100 miles northwest of Anchorage. We wore waders, light rain slickers and of course, that .44 magnum. Then we set off upriver, hoping to explore two feeder streams and another lake. We were looking for trout or grayling.

The forest was so thick with spruce, aspen and brush that the only trails were bear paths, which looked like tunnels in the vegetation. We stayed clear of them—after all, in the forest you could walk right into a bear without warning.

So we hiked upriver, knee-deep in water, where we could see up and down the stream, so any bear could be spotted easily. The sockeye salmon, with green heads and deep red humpbacks, were

so thick in some pools that you had to consciously avoid stepping on them. Fishermen are rarely excited by sockeye, since they are reluctant to take a fly and often are snagged by accident.

Occasionally we'd see that same sight again: a dead salmon along the river with a single giant bite taken out of it.

"I sure hope we don't run into a griz," said my companion, an Alaskan fishing guide named Randy. "There are a lot of black bears around, but they'll run. With a griz, you never know."

That was when I remembered a family legend. "In the '40s, my grandmother was hiking near Lake Louise in the Canadian Rockies," I told him. "A grizzly grabbed her, squeezed her in his arms for awhile, then tossed her aside. She played dead, and other than some scratches, she got out with nothing more than a scare."

"Sometimes a griz will false charge," Randy said. "They'll look you in the eye from 40 yards, then gallop straight at you and veer off at 10 feet. Sometimes they keep coming. Some say they like to hear the crunch noises when they bite somebody's head."

Thoughts like that can make you trigger-happy. But the last thing in the world you want to do is shoot a grizzly if you don't have to. Even with a well-placed slug from a shotgun at point blank range, the big guy is apt to get his hands on you before he drops. Every year, though, somebody shoots a griz, then gets grabbed, bit and maybe sent to the Happy Hunting Ground.

If a grizzly grabs you, and you play it by the book, you're supposed to go limp and silent. After a few squeezes, they're supposed to lose interest. At that point, they'll bury you in dirt and tree limbs. Later, you can sneak off. But you never know. If you have the chance, get up a tree, at least 15 feet high. Grizzlies are so big and weigh so much that they can't climb trees—their claws can't hold their weight.

Even where grizzly populations are significant, like in Yellowstone and Glacier national parks, or in Alaska and the Northwest Territories, the chance of meeting up with one is low. Most patrol a huge range, and if they get a whiff of you or hear you, they will likely avoid you.

But not always. Every once in a while, man meets bear. At that point, the behavior of either party is unpredictable.

"There was this guide named Jake who got false charged twice in five years," Randy said. "Then last year, his clients came running up to him, yelling about a giant bear chasing them. So he walked right up to the bear and started yelling at it, figuring it would leave. Instead the bear took two steps toward him and swatted his head off with one blow."

I was wondering whether or not to believe that tale when we came up on another big footprint, about eight inches across. Some Eskimos say you can size a bear by its print, adding the number one to the width of the print, then converting it into feet. For instance, an eight-inch print would belong to a nine-foot bear. Some other Eskimos say that's a lot of bunk.

We hiked up two tributaries of the Talachulitna and found more sockeye salmon, but no trout or grayling. The latter are the fish that anglers prize. They'll hit a well-presented fly or spinner and they're hard-fighting fish on light tackle. Our hike continued upriver, past a beaver dam, and eventually we reached a small lake that fed the stream. Maybe this would hold grayling. But no, we just found a few sockeyes that had jumped the beaver dam.

There were no grizzlies either, at least not any we saw. "Just another day exploring the Alaska wilds," Randy said with a laugh.

Then he looked down and saw a bear print, a huge one, practically the size of a dinner plate.

Heh, heh, heh. There is no such thing as just another day up here. The grizzlies make you think, make you wonder: "Is there a bear around the bend?"

Imagine a secret fishing hole where bald eagles patrol the sky, the sea is a quiet paradise, and coastal fishing spots abound where it is difficult to hold a fishing rod and count "one, two, three" without hooking a big halibut.

You want to talk about big halibut? Salmon? The physical struggle of hooking one of these monsters can practically clean the cholesterol right out of your bloodstream.

We're talking about Ketchikan, located on Alaska's southeastern coast. It rarely snows here, even in winter, and the magic of flight can take anybody from the continental U.S. to Ketchikan, then on to the wilderness via amphibious airplane in just one day, and for people on the West Coast, in a matter of three to six hours.

Situated on a remote island on Alaska's Alexander Archipelago is Waterfall Resort, the jumpoff point for some of the most extraordinary fishing expeditions one could imagine in this hemisphere, as well as a first-class setting for an exotic vacation.

It was a warm June day, with a clear sky and a calm sea. My guide, Harris Natkong, a full-blooded Haida Indian, swung the boat into a cove of one of the many islands off the Alaskan coast, then turned the engine off. "This is Addington Cove," said Natkong. "After today, you will never forget it."

I tied an eight-inch chrome bar on my fishing line and plunked it over the side. The sea is so clear here that you can watch it descend for more than 50 feet into the water. The lure clunked on the bottom 90 feet down, and then—boom! Halibut. Just like that. A good one, maybe 25 pounds. My partner, Jim Martin, was tussling with one as well, a 20-pounder.

"We throw these back," said Natkong. "Too small." An hour later, we had not gone five seconds without a hookup. Just try counting to three.

"I learned about Cape Addington, and fished it the first day I could walk," said Natkong, who was born and reared on a nearby island. "I was born to the sea and fishing is my life. It was my father's life. He showed me this spot."

Just then a seagull flew over, and Natkong laughed. "Indian legend says that white eyes come back as seagulls," he said. "We come back as ravens."

In the Indian villages along the Alaskan coast, the tales of the giant halibut, 300- and 400-pounders, are often told. In one story, a young Indian battled a 120-pounder with rod and reel from a 16-foot skiff for hours before the huge fish could be brought alongside the boat. The man readied a small gaff hook, complete with a wrist wrap, and caught the fish. But the halibut suddenly went berserk and surged back down, pulling the man out of the boat and deep into the sea.

"We never saw that boy again," said Natkong. Another time, a 200-pounder was caught and brought aboard, then flopped and walloped a man and broke his leg. "We have taken halibut, and they have taken us," Natkong added.

However, after two hours, the scorecard was something like Fisherman 60, Halibut 0, although all of the fish except one were released. The 20-pounders were biting so fast, however, that the bigger fellows never had a chance to strike. I've never seen anything like it. But I knew giant ones had to be down there, so I tried something unique, perhaps bizarre.

For a twist, I cut a 10-inch fillet off a rockfish, and managed to skewer it on the largest hook aboard for one giant hunk of bait. I let it down to the bottom and immediately started getting bites. For 30 minutes, it was like holding a shock stick. You could feel the 20-pounders tugging at it, biting it, trying to eat it, yet they were not large enough to be hooked. Then…wham! That bait was hit so hard that the rod was almost ripped out of my hands. No foolin'. I leaned back and set the hook, and you could feel the immense weight of the fish below.

"Big one," Natkong said. "Big one."

For an hour, that halibut dragged us for a half mile, ripped 40 yards of line at a time, and showed the kind of bulldog strength that might break a horse. It felt like a telephone pole with a jet drive, with tremendous, powerful dives, one after the other. I grappled with it for an hour, my body starting to seize up as if I'd been powerlifting weights at a gym. Well into the second hour, we first saw its dark shape in the sea. We couldn't believe its size. It looked like a spacecraft out of *Star Wars*, hovering below us, much bigger than a man.

Later at the dock, we needed a forklift to move it about. It measured over six feet long and bottomed out the scale at 100 pounds.

You know those giant salmon that are most often advertised in the Alaska brochures? We caught a 53-pounder that gave proof to the legends, and fishermen from throughout the world will come here, hoping for such a fish. What they might not know, but they should, is that also awaiting them is the best halibut fishing in the world.

Just try counting to three at Addington Cove.

The Alaskan air tasted pure and smelled of pines and fish. The river pushed gently against my waders, and I stabled myself in the current and began casting.

Zip—I cast to the left of a rock, then twitched the streamer. Nothing. I raised the fly rod back, picking up the line, false casting twice to gain control, then laid the streamer just to the right of the rock. Twitch-twitch. Nothing. *Zip*—I shot the streamer to a deep pocket behind a big boulder. I twitch-twitched again on the fly. How can they resist?

Just then a swirl the size of a big washtub encircled the fly, and an instant later, the line tightened. I set the hook. The rod bent down and with a jolt, a silver salmon came three feet out of the water, thrashed the surface into foam, then ripped off 30 yards of line, all in the flash of a few moments. Ten minutes later, the fish was led to the shoreline, unhooked, and it darted away to its friends.

Some say this is the ultimate, on the river with a fly rod, casting for wild silver salmon, getting the thrill of your life and knowing it. Suddenly every cell in your body feels alive.

A river that is a legend for its silver salmon run is the Talachulitna River, called the "Tal" for short, some 70 to 100 miles by bush plane out of Anchorage. This river curls 200 miles to the ocean, feeding through a maze of other streams. Salmon? You've never seen so many. The Tal attracts five different summer runs of salmon—kings, silvers, sockeyes, pinks and chums. The kings are the biggest, the silvers the most exciting and the sockeyes the most plentiful. Some of the nearby feeder creeks have a sprinkling of Dolly Varden trout and Arctic grayling.

Out trip was timed to catch the end of the sockeye salmon run and the beginning of the silver run. Sockeyes turn a brilliant red tipped by a green head while on their migratory journey. The fish pack so closely together in some pools that the river will seem to turn from green to red. Sockeyes, averaging eight to 12 pounds, are fighters that pack a punch. But sometimes they are so thick that you even snag them by accident while retrieving.

Such is not the case with silvers, which are more elusive, powerful and exciting fish. With silvers you get it all. Acrobats with power. Sizzle and steak.

Any style of fishing will do. Spinning outfits, steelhead gear, fly rods? Take your pick. We tried them all. Newcomer or seasoned angler, it makes no difference.

The bush plane landed on an Alaskan lake, fed by the headwaters of the Tal, the destination for thousands of salmon. In a matter of minutes, we were out of the plane, into our waders and waist deep in the river. On my second cast, I had a hookup and watched the fish rip 30 feet of line, reel spinning in my hands, before it threw the hook.

"Did you see that?"

"Yeeee-ow!" shouted my companion, Earl Bradford, casting nearby. Before Bradford could raise his eyebrows, he had hooked up with a beauty.

It jumped immediately, a big silver, then zigged, zagged and jumped again. Bradford "yeeee-owed" a couple more times, then the fish ran 40 yards straight away, jumped and hit the water with a big surge and popped the line.

"I blew it," said Bradford, looking like a puppy dog that just lost its first bone. "Got excited, clamped down on the line. Too much pressure, popped it off."

But a few minutes later he had another hookup. "Yeeee-ow!" echoed across the mountain.

Every salmon feels like a prize. I used a No. 6 fly rod, which is a rod more suited to rainbow trout than salmon, casting streamers. Rigging with a spinning rod or steelhead-type gear and casting spoons has the same result: Salmon get hooked. If a fish gets off, no problem. Just take another cast, my friend.

When you're burned out on catching monsters, you can try the old Judd Lake Jump. That's where you get in a red-hot sauna and sweat until you can scarcely breathe. Then you run outside and take a flying leap into Judd Lake and turn into a human icicle.

As for Bradford, he says he'll "stick to the salmon."

Deep in the frontier of Alaska is a fish named Jargo, a rainbow trout that can make anglers yowl like a lone wolf baying at the moon.

Jargo lives in a stream called Little Bear Creek, set in Katmai National Park. This is a wildland of open tundra bordered by rows of glacial peaks and the Valley of 10,000 Smokes, where the most violent volcanoes in the world are found. That's fitting, you see, because Jargo is equally explosive. I've seen him and hooked him. So have a few others.

"There may be no rainbow trout in the world like that one," said Ed Rice of Vancouver, Washington, who has fished in dozens of countries, chasing after the world's fightingest fish, and has spent 67 weeks in Alaska. "Last year I had him on for 20 minutes. He's absolutely huge, strong and smart. I tried everything, but that fish got away on me. I haven't been able to stop thinking about him."

It was Rice who first told me about Jargo. I was blueprinting an adventure to hunt down giant rainbow trout, no matter where it took me or at what cost, and had narrowed the destinations to Argentina, Chile, New Zealand and Alaska. Then Rice told me about Little Bear Creek and the trout that live there. A good friend, flyfishing guru Mike Wolverton, of Idaho, had also heard about Jargo and was primed for the quest. Wolverton has caught all salmon species on the fly, as well as sailfish and marlin. On an expedition to Belize, he landed a giant permit, a rare, elusive species of fish.

"Jargo," he said simply, "is different from other fish." As he spoke, Mike's typically kind, relaxed eyes suddenly narrowed into a pair of laser beams. Jargo can do that to you.

For a base camp, we returned to Kulik Lodge, and we arranged for special trips to Little Bear Creek. To hone my skills, I arrived a day early, by jet to Anchorage, then by twin Piper Navajo to a wilderness dirt airstrip, then by float plane to the Alagnak River with guide Wayne Hansen. After landing, I waded out from a sand bar and started casting, letting the fly drift downstream.

Bang! A salmon hit that fly, jumped three times, and then took off downstream like a pit bull chasing a meat truck. It didn't stop for 70 yards, my fly reel handle spinning around at warp speed, whacking my thumb on every turn. What a fish: It darted upstream, downstream, power dived, jumped 10 times, but after 20 minutes, it was mine.

It was silver salmon, just under 10 pounds, a perfect warm-up for Jargo. The river was loaded with salmon, and these fish haven't exactly taken smart lessons.

On the other hand, Jargo has. In fact, Jargo administers them. The next day, Wolverton and I flew out to Little Bear Creek to sign up for class.

The flight lifted off and we gained altitude under a flat gray overcast sky, a few sprinkles of rain dancing on the windshield. Below Gibraltar Peak to the east, we spotted a herd of caribou, the males with huge racks, like reindeer. Bright red Alaskan fireweed enlivened the green tundra, and we surveyed endless miles of open range, flecked with small ponds and gouged by a few rivers.

"There's the Little Bear River," Wolverton said. His eyes had that wolf-like stare again, just like the first time he talked about Jargo.

We cruised the river, about 800 feet over the top, getting a bald eagle's view of the stream from the airplane. Visible below were clusters of spawning sockeye salmon, packed in groups of 75 to 100 fish, sometimes more. It was just what we were looking for. You see, when salmon spawn, they bury their eggs in the river gravel, but some of the eggs always slip downstream. Big rainbow trout will wait downstream of the spawning salmon, sitting almost motionless in the current, and then pick the eggs off as they drift by.

We landed the float plane on a small pond in the tundra, then hiked for several miles. The Alaskan tundra has a mushy cushion to it, and to make better time, we picked out a worn bear trail, then followed it toward the stream. We reached an overlook and gazed up and down Little Bear Creek.

"We have company," Wolverton said.

Upstream were two big Alaskan brown bears, both of them nailing a sockeye salmon now and then, taking a big bite out of the roe cavity, stripping the fish of its flesh. In a week, we spotted about 25 Alaskan browns, including big females with sets of cubs. They kept their distance, more interested in the salmon than us, and we kept ours.

From that overlook, using Polaroid glasses, we were able to discern the dark silhouettes of giant rainbow trout holding motionless in the current, well below the schools of spawning salmon.

"There they are," Wolverton said. "Jargo is out there somewhere."

This was the strategy: We'd fish one trout at a time, spotting its silhouette in the river, stalking it, then casting to it, using egg-like patterns with a single, barbless hook. Then we'd hike on, spotting and stalking, keeping an eye out for Mr. Griz.

After a few days with this strategy, my biggest trout was an eight-pounder, Jargo Jr., measuring 28 inches long, with the blackest spots and brightest red stripe you've ever seen. Wolverton had caught several even bigger ones, in the 30-inch, 10-pound class. Each fish was carefully released unharmed, resuscitated in the river current if necessary.

One morning I was knee-deep in the river, holding a big trout by the tail, pulling it back and forth in the current to revive it. Right then, I felt the shadow of a bear. I turned, and charging upstream was a grizzly! His shoulders were so big that you could see his muscles rolling, and with each bounding jump, he made giant splashes. His mouth was open, his eyes stared straight at me and he was galloping right toward me. I let the fish go and sprinted for the shore. Play dead? You gotta be kidding. I climbed up a bluff as if propelled by rocket boosters, then turned and looked back. In an apparent seige of madness, the bear swirled around and with his giant paws, slapped at the water in every direction in a fifteen-foot circle. I got the message loud and clear—it was his spot, not mine. I hiked a half-mile upriver before deciding to fish again.

You might ask why anyone would fish with bears always looming nearby in the bush. Jargo, that's why.

A few days later, I waded across the creek to a small island, and was stalking a narrow chute when the sun suddenly popped clear of a cloud—and just 30 feet in front of me was the dark shadow of a trout that looked like a sunken log. I stared closer, the polarized sunglasses cutting through the glare. Log? More like a submarine. Jargo? Maybe.

As I stared, I could hear my heart racing. The big trout shifted position a few inches to one side, then moved right back, as if picking off a passing salmon egg. "He's feeding," I said aloud to nobody. "It's Jargo and he's feeding."

As gently as possible, almost afraid to breathe, I cast upstream, the fly line landing softly on the river surface, and watched the scene unfold: The trout was motionless, then moved over a few inches and grabbed the passing egg pattern. I set the hook; the rod bent—I had him! But the big trout just lay there.

For two minutes, nothing happened. The trout didn't budge. I couldn't move him off his spot, and he wasn't interested in anything else, not even a small tussle.

"So this is Jargo, eh?" I muttered. "Big deal."

At that exact moment, the trout started to swim across the stream, then darted toward me. Apparently, it was so big that it had not even realized it was hooked. But now the trout knew, and it did not like it.

Right in front of me, not 20 feet away, the trout jumped clear of the water, three feet high, and then landed with a giant *whap*. It was Jargo! In the next 20 seconds, Jargo bolted downstream, the line screaming out of my reel, and it never stopped.

Suddenly, Jargo was gone. I looked down at my reel and all my line was gone, too. My knot had popped right off. I've never had a fish do that before.

I felt a strange mixture of awe and disappointment, and I walked downstream toward Wolverton to tell him what happened. Oddly, Wolverton was already walking toward me, and before I could say a word, he started talking.

"The strangest thing just happened," Wolverton said. "This line came floating by me, so I grabbed it and there was this giant trout on. I held on for a few seconds, then the line broke."

I just pointed at my reel.

"Jargo?"

"Jargo."

A week later, on the way out of the wilderness, I flew over the stream again, and looked down at Little Bear Creek with piqued irony. I felt both a sense of loss and a sense of gain, then smiled at the thought of that fish. There is a mighty trout down there, you see, that may be just too much fish for anybody.

For a brochure detailing lodges available in Katmai National Park, write Katmailand, 4700 Aircraft Drive, Anchorage, AK 99502, or phone (800) 544-0551.

For a brochure describing Katmai National Park, write Superintendent, P.O. Box 7, King Salmon, AK 99613.

Abe Cuanang pulls the gory remains of a sea lion from the water after a shark attacked the animal near Abe's boat

Pacific
SHARK HUNT

Face to Face with a Great White

❖

In the depths of sleep, I was dreaming that I had fallen in the ocean and giant Great White sharks were attacking me. I was punching them, trying to fight them off.

Then I awoke in a sudden fury, sweating, my arms and legs twitching. It was 2 a.m. An hour later, still wide awake, I got up and headed for the boat. You see, we were going fishing for Great Whites. As I cruised down the empty highway, I couldn't get that dream out of my mind.

At the dock, Ski Ratto and his brother, Robert, had already arrived, also an hour early. "I slept about an hour," Ski Ratto said. "This is getting to me. I keep thinking about how big they are."

A few minutes later, up drives Abe Cuanang, also ready for the trip. "Couldn't sleep," he said. Great White sharks have a way of doing that to you. Every one of us, faced with the prospect of tangling with a man-eater, not only could not sleep, but found ourselves at the dock in the middle of the night, consumed by the passion of the adventure.

It wasn't long before our two skiffs, 17-foot Boston Whalers, were whipping across San Francisco Bay, heading out to sea. After passing the orange glow of the Golden Gate Bridge, the Pacific Ocean was as dark as the sockets of a skull.

I had been fishing for Great White sharks for several years, but lately I had teamed up with the brothers Cuanang, two of the finest saltwater anglers and boatmen in the country. They were Abe and Angelo, anglers extraordinaire. It was the Cuanangs who developed a system of trolling a hoochie baited with pork rind for lingcod and rockfish, a rare but effective way to fill a boat with fish. Fishing in separate skiffs, they had been catching 700 to 1,000 pounds of fish per trip in a week, then selling the fish on the commercial market. Together we hoped to catch something a little more elusive.

If there was ever a day when a fisherman might hook and fight a 17-foot, 4,000-pound Great White with rod and reel, this was it. We knew the huge fish was there, waiting, eating whatever it wanted. One that big has never been caught by rod and reel in history, not anywhere and not by anybody. We didn't plan on trying to kill a fish like that, but to go one-on-one with it, then cut it free. Man versus man-eater.

The chances never seemed better. Just the day before, Ski Ratto had been fishing for rockfish and lingcod, and when he turned on his depth finder, the bottom registered 120 feet deep. But suddenly, on the screen, the bottom of the ocean appeared to be rising to 80 feet, then 50 feet, then 40 feet. But the boat had not moved. Impossible? A malfunction? No: It was a shark under the boat, a fish so gigantic that the electronic sonar impulses sent by the depth finder were bouncing off the shark and reading it as the ocean bottom.

Later, just as Ratto was bringing a small rockfish aboard, he looked down and saw it. A Great White four feet across at the head was looking right at him, just two feet from the boat, about a foot below the surface.

"He had a giant eye that looked right at me," Ratto said. "A strange feeling went through me like nothing I have ever felt. I panicked and gave the boat full throttle and got the hell out of there."

It was the seventh Great White episode experienced among Ratto, Abe Cuanang and me in a 10-day span, including twice watching 600-pound sea lions get annihilated in less than two minutes. So we were back, this time prepared.

We arrived at our secret spot just as daylight peaked out from the east. First we had to catch our "bait."

We dangled 16-ounce chrome jigs along the ocean bottom, yanking the rods now and then to make the lures flutter. Bang! A hit! It wasn't long before a 12-pound lingcod came aboard. Just about the right size for bait. In less than half an hour, we had caught several.

We moved the boats to the prime area, then hooked the live lingcod through the back with a hook about 10 inches long and four-and-a-half inches wide. Clamped to the hook was three feet of chain, then 12 feet of four separate 1,000-pound test strand wire for leader. We had heavy big-game tuna rods with roller guides, and for reels, Penn Internationals with 500 yards of 130-pound test line.

We set two lines out at 70 feet deep, the chain providing all the weight necessary to get it there, and let the live lingcod swim about. We set two other lines about 40 yards off the boat, about 30 feet deep, with large red balloons tied on as "bobbers." Kind of like fishing at a pond for bluegills, right? Well, not quite. One "bait" we used was a 60-pound bat ray Abe Cuanang had caught in San Francisco Bay and saved for the Big Day.

There were no other boats in view for miles. The ocean had just the slightest roll to it and our only companions were passing gulls, murres and shearwaters. Occasionally a few sea lions would cruise by, then start hopping across the sea like trained porpoises, then jump like penguins out of the water and onto an island. We all saw this and immediately knew why.

"The big guy is down there," said Cuanang. "There's no other reason for them to hop like that." You see, when a Great White is cruising around, even sea lions are smart enough to get the heck out of the water.

We were all quite tense, but after years of planning and testing various rigs, it seemed we had everything in order. The two boats were tied together with a quick release. From below, their shadow would appear to be a large square platform, not an elephant seal or anything else a shark might want to eat. That is why surfers get mistaken for shark food.

We were going over our plans one last time. If there was a pick-up on a bait, the boats would be released, and after setting the hook, the boat would be gunned 75 yards to get immediate distance between us and the shark. "Got it?" asked Abe.

Before anyone could answer, there was a violent jerk on one of the rods, the one hooked with a three-and-a-half-foot lingcod swimming 60 feet deep. For the flash of an instant, we all froze.

Then Abe Cuanang, who was closest, grabbed it. His eyes looked as if they were going to pop out of his head. Later, Ratto said I had the same look.

"I can feel his head jerking side to side with the bait," Cuanang shouted. "He's eating it!"

He put the reel on free-spool and the shark started to swim off, straight ahead of the boat. The line peeled off the revolving spool. I was just about to shout "Strike!" when Cuanang put the reel in gear to do exactly that. But nothing happened.

"Something weird's happening," Cuanang said. Then it hit him. "He's swimming for the boat! He's swimming for the boat!"

Cuanang reeled with ferocity to pick up the slack. But when the line tightened, the shark was gone, and so was the bait.

We all looked at the bare hook. The only sound was a seal barking in the distance.

"He robbed our bait," Ratto said.

Well, somewhere out there in the briny deep was a Great White shark with a lingcod in its belly.

How big was he? Likely bigger than anyone can imagine.

A day before one of our shark hunts, one of the biggest Great White sharks ever documented washed up at Año Nuevo State Park on the San Mateo County coastline. The shark was 18 feet long, weighed an estimated 4,500 pounds, and had a mouth big enough to eat a man in one bite and two gulps.

It may have been the same Great White that was responsible for two deadly attacks in the same area. At nearby Pigeon Point, an abalone diver was nearly bitten in half and killed by a shark, and in Monterey Bay, a surfer was ripped right off his board and killed.

"We hypothesized that a 20-footer killed the kid in Monterey," said John McCosker of Steinhart Aquarium in San Francisco, one of the world's leading shark experts. He had a look of awe in his eyes.

"How did you estimate the size?" I asked him.

"We compared the tooth marks on the surfboard to shark jaws in the museum (at Steinhart), jaws of known length, comparing the space between the teeth. On that basis, we figured it was an 18-, 19- or 20-footer."

When the Great White's massive corpse washed up at Año Nuevo, park rangers first thought it was an elephant seal, since they breed in the area, until they got a closer look. The shark was measured, photographed and filmed—and Steinhart's McCosker was contacted. He immediately arranged a scientific study and autopsy of the creature.

"But when we arrived the next morning, the shark was gone," McCosker said. "The high tide at night washed it back out to sea. It was the big one that got away."

When shown photographs and videotape of the shark, McCosker and other experts were astounded by the size of the fish. The only people I know who have looked eye-to-eye with 4,000-pound sharks are McCosker and Al Giddings of Ocean Quest.

"We estimated it at 4,500 to 5,000 pounds, a huge female," Giddings told me. "Imagine that." Giddings is a world-renowned underwater photographer who has swam unprotected with 18-footers and returned with amazing photographs.

One of the few people who documented the shark was Año Nuevo Park Ranger Chuck Scimeca. "I came over a rise and saw it on Cascade Beach," Scimeca said. "I got out there and couldn't believe it. The bulk—I'll never forget it. Its head was four feet wide."

The documentation that sharks of this size roam so near the Bay Area should shock the public into realizing that danger quietly inhabits such nearby waters. There have been more shark attacks off the Bay Area coast than anywhere else in the world. McCosker tries to keep track of each one.

Scientists call the area bordered by Año Nuevo to the south, the Farallon Islands to the west, and Bodega Bay to the north the "Red Triangle" or the "Farallon Triangle." Great Whites live here year round, feeding on abundant populations of sea lions and sea elephants.

A Great White tagging program was directed at the Farallon Islands by Peter Klimley of Scripps Institute. He tagged several sharks, including two 17-footers, in a 45-minute span. As many as 13 or 14 of this size have been documented at one time.

When sharks like these—sharks that weigh 3,500 or 4,000 pounds—decide to eat, they eat. And they are not always picky. In fact, Klimley's Zodiac rubber boat was bit and sunk by a Great White. At the time of the attack, nobody was in the boat, which had been used to shuttle scientists from the island to research vessels. "I'm thankful for that," he told me.

"More adult white sharks are documented (in the Triangle) than in any other location on the West Coast," Klimley said. "I am a believer. That was my rubber boat that got sunk."

Two Great White sharks were tagged with electronic instruments, allowing the man-eaters to be monitored for daily behavior, traveling range and how they are affected by various environmental factors. Tracking instruments were embedded in big hunks of meat, which the sharks swallowed. The instruments then transmitted ultrasonic "pingers," tracked by the scientists, until the ultrasonic pings suddenly disappeared. The scientists never picked up the sound wave again and they never knew what happened.

The key to the expanding population of Great Whites is the Marine Mammal Protection Act of 1974. Since sea lions and elephant seals have been protected, they have provided a much larger food source for Great Whites. In turn, baby Great Whites started having much higher survival rates in the early 1980s. Now in the '90s there are so many Great Whites that someone gets bit nearly every year, usually a surfer dressed up to look just like shark food.

Considerable dispute rages over the size of the largest Great White in history. A 36-footer in England and a 29-footer in the Azores are the largest documented. The largest Great White ever weighed was 7,300 pounds and measured 21 feet, three inches long. It was snarled in a net off Cuba in the 1930s. However, there are tales of 40- and 50-footers.

"No doubt larger ones have been seen," said scientist McCosker. "We may have a few off our own coast...It can give you the chills."

The abundance of Great White sharks off the Bay Area has become critical to keep the marine ecosystem in balance. This is how the chain works: Because sharks eat sea lions, and sea lions eat fish, more sharks mean fewer sea lions and more fish. Marine mammals, such as sea lions, eat five times as many fish as are taken by sport and commercial fishermen put together. Thus, if you remove the sharks, the sea lions have no enemies—and, ultimately, fisheries can be damaged by increased sea lion predation.

That is why it is illegal to kill sharks. As scary as they appear, their survival is vital. But you won't find me dangling my legs from a surfboard.

The idea that "I might just get eaten today" sat in the back of my mind every time we went fishing for Great White sharks. For good reason. We had seen sharks big enough to eat a person in one bite, with mouths the size of a barrel, huge chainsaw-like teeth and awesome bodies. But there we were again, cruising out from San Francisco to the Gulf of the Farallones in relatively tiny Boston

Whaler skiffs, driven by the fascination and excitement that comes with Great White encounters.

We'd been close before. One day, as the boat cruised at trolling speed, Angelo's rod suddenly stopped cold, like he'd snagged bottom. Then the snag moved.

"I think I got the big guy," Angelo said.

The "big guy" is Mr. You Know Who. Angelo leaned back on the rod with everything he had, and the fish didn't budge an inch. Then it swam a bit, moving the boat. With lingcod gear, that shark did not even know it was hooked—it was like trying to stop a freight train with a roadblock. Then the big shark started to swim off, actually towing the boat at five knots, creating a small wake, an unbelievable sight.

But suddenly, the line went limp. Angelo, his heart still jumping around in his chest, reeled in his line—and found the hook had been straightened.

"You must have snagged him accidentally," Abe shouted from his own boat, "maybe in the back."

How big would a fish have to be to tow an ocean-going boat? How big? It made us tremble.

That fish was never seen. But others have made up for that.

A small Great White, about a 300-pounder, came up and swiped a lingcod right off the line just as Angelo was about to bring it aboard.

"It was so close I could have touched him with my hands," Angelo said. "I looked him right in the eye. I think my heart skipped a beat. I just about went into shock."

A much bigger one also stole a lingcod off Abe's line, also just under the boat. This shark was gigantic, about a 17-footer—which is about the size of the Great White in the movie *Jaws*. Through the clear water, the shark was spinning and chewing the fish.

"They're getting bolder," said Abe, with a strange mix of nervous laughter, fear and excitement in his voice.

In another episode the same week, a Great White hammered a

sea lion right on the surface, completely ravaging the 650-pound mammal in less than two minutes. Just as Abe was cruising up, the tip of the shark's dorsal fin disappeared below the surface. Another time, a Great White plucked a sea lion right out of the rolling surf, then disappeared. Only a reddish tint in the water was left behind, and that too quickly vanished.

The biggest surprise was that getting Great Whites to strike our bait was a mysterious and elusive gamble. Because the water is so clear this far out to sea, our chain may have been spooking them. We tried painting it black to reduce any glare, which seemed to help.

Crazy? Yeah, we were a little crazy. But we weren't crazy enough to go out without the know-how to accomplish our goal. We wanted to fight them. It is the ultimate in the world of fishing—playing a 4,000-pound fish that can eat you, then cutting it free.

Fast forward to Bodega Bay.

Jim Siegle hadn't said a word for 20 minutes. Alongside, Dick Pool stared ahead across miles of open ocean, looking toward Tomales Point.

The big Wellcraft was cutting a clean wake across the open ocean, and with the throttle at cruise speed, I pointed the boat to where we hoped to hook a Great White. The wind was light, not more than five knots, with only a few murres and cormorants sprinkled about the sea, a flawless calm.

"Everything seems perfect," said Siegle.

"That's what scares me," I answered. "Sometimes when everything seems perfect, you're about ready to take a fall."

"I'd thought about that myself," noted Dick Pool.

The three of us had planned this trip for a long time: Great White sharks had been spotted at the mouth of Tomales Bay. We were heading out hoping to tangle with one.

Siegle, who passed away in late 1993, started with a curious fascination about what he called "Nature's perfect eating machines," and then developed a system that has become the standard for shark fishing along the West Coast. Pool is the renowned underwater TV master, who has perfected filming fish striking baits, and in the process has been able to invent new techniques for salmon and albacore fishing.

The three of us, longtime friends from many expeditions, suddenly realized one day that each of us shared the same fixation about catching a Great White. We then spent hours and hours talking strategy, developing rigs, and ultimately, fishing together on the most exhilarating fishing trips imaginable.

"Great White sharks aren't really such bad fellows," Siegle said, "except that they eat people now and then."

It was no accident that the mouth of Tomales Bay was our destination. It was here that a giant Great White came up behind the boat and breached like a whale, then with its head out of the water, began barking like a dog at us as it gulped air. I guess it wanted a bone. "Lunch served yet?"

When we reached the spot, Siegle opened one of four rubber garbage cans; each was filled to the brim with all matter of fish carcasses, obtained from a commercial fish buyer. Siegle then started laying a chum line, feeding the carcasses into a grinder, which leaves a trail of fish bits and chunks in the water, along with a light floating slick from the fish oil.

"The smell is unbelievable!" he shouted.

"Ooh, how about those three- and four-day-old mushy ones," said Pool. The smell of rotten fish is so wicked that after a full whiff, you might find yourself doing some chumming yourself from a five-point stance.

As the chum line was being laid, I reviewed our equipment. For tackle, we used heavy, world-class rods, reels and line, most of which was supplied by Siegle. He obtained the heaviest rod Sabre makes, rated at 130-pound test and equipped with giant roller guides, and with Penn's largest reel, a size 16/0 (nearly 10 inches across). It was loaded with 700 yards of 130-pound Ande monofilament, the standard for world-class line. The rig was so heavy you practically needed a hoist to strap it on. To support it, you needed a full shoulder and back harness, to which the rod and reel were connected. We also used Penn International reels set up on heavy tuna rods, 80-pound class, which were a lot easier to handle.

The shoulder harness represents a touch of danger when shark fishing. If you hook the Big Guy, get a backlash in the reel, and then the shark takes off on a power run, you could be pulled right into the water because you are connected to the rod by the harness. That is why we always kept a knife at the ready.

Pool always made sure the knife was sharp. "Now if I start getting pulled into the water, one of you guys had better cut the line," he ordered. "Imagine hooking up with a 5,000-pounder, getting pulled into the water, then having him turn around and come for you."

The terminal rigging was an awesome sight. We used giant hooks, 18/0 when we could get them, with chain and five-strand wires. Siegle designed the rigging, using no knots for connectors, but only wire clamps that could take 10,000 pounds of stress.

For bait, we used whatever was available for each trip. As on my trips with the Cuanang brothers, we sometimes used a live lingcod, about a 15- or 20-pounder. Another very good bait was a ray in the 40- to 50-pound class. At times, we also used two or three stickle-back sharks (dogfish), or combinations of small sharks and rockfish.

But on this escapade, we had a different strategy. Pool made a trip to a rural tallow works, where a fellow named Jake was fasci-nated with our adventure. He gave us several bags of dried blood to feed our chum line, and also a stillborn calf for bait. Jake must have been a little crazy, just like us.

After the bait plopped in the water, Pool rigged his underwater camera from a downrigger, so we could watch everything that happened down there. The picture came in quite clear, thanks to the calm day. The calm was a prerequisite to the trip, we had all agreed. "First, we must have a calm ocean," Siegle said. "Imagine a rough ocean. You lose your balance and then fall in by accident. All Whitey would see would be your legs kicking back and forth as he came up the chum line. It gives me nightmares."

We also worked out precise emergency teamwork maneuvers: Keeping a knife nearby at all times if cutting the line is necessary, having the boat prepared to get the heck out of there if the shark attacks and tries to ramrod us, and having a shotgun aboard with deer slugs at the ready.

"Let's keep the chum line going," Siegle directed, and this time it was Pool's turn to hold his nose and reach into the mushy pot of deteriorating carcasses.

So we chummed and we waited. You might think that sharks of all kinds would respond instantly to the chum line. That just plain never happens. Only rarely in the fall when blue sharks are more common has there been even a tremor of visible response. Regardless, we kept at it, because we had learned that a Great White works on instinct, and we hoped to inspire his predatory instinct with the smell of blood.

"The hope is that if a shark is in the area, the chum line may get him in the biting mood," Siegle said. "We could always dangle our feet in the water to do the same, of course, but for now I have decided against that strategy."

The amount of waiting can be agonizing, especially for people who are accustomed to quick results. But wait you must, knowing all the while that a typical Great White off California is a 12-footer that weighs about 1,500 to 1,700 pounds. You also realize that there are several 15- to 17-footers in the 2,500- to 3,000-pound class, and that there is the remote possibility that a 19- or 20-footer weighing perhaps 5,000 pounds will be the next fish swimming under your small boat.

"We know they're here," Siegle said. "The question is, do they know that we're here, too?"

The answer came immediately. A dark shadow appeared on one side of the TV screen, then vanished.

"Look! Did you see that?" Pool asked.

We were tense, too tense to talk. Without a word, Siegle grabbed the big game rod, hoping for a chance to set the hook. Pool and I stared into the TV screen, and then again, on the left side of the screen, a blurred grayish shadow moved across.

"I wish I could focus it, but with this underwater camera, the focal point is fixed. There's no way to tell how big it is until he gets close to the bait. Then he'll be in focus."

The next half hour was the most excruciating I can remember spending on a boat. We knew there was something down there, something big. We knew our bait was waiting for it, that our chum line was now dispersing fish scent for miles.

But at the rod, there was no tug, no nibble, just silence.

"He doesn't want to bite," Siegle said eventually, shaking his head, exasperated that the showdown had come to this.

"Even though everything is giant, it's still fishing," Pool answered. "Giant tackle, giant hook, giant bait, giant sharks, but just like fishing for anything, you can't always get them to bite."

"Maybe he's full," I said with a laugh.

Maybe not.

A few weeks later, Pool heard a bizarre story about a fellow named Hank who had been salmon fishing near the same spot. He called Siegle and me together to share the story with us.

Hank hooked what he figured was the biggest salmon of his life off Tomales Point when a Great White came up and bit it in half. The half of fish that Hank reeled in weighed 25 pounds.

"He was enraged," Pool said, "and the next day returned to the same spot."

Hank poured all matter of fish carcasses in the water, and after an hour, Whitey returned to the scene of the crime. Hank responded by tossing out the remaining half salmon on a giant hook—which was connected by cable to a power winch he'd taken from his four-wheel drive. Well, sure enough, the shark took the bait, and Hank winched the shark right up to the back of the boat, and then started firing at it with a deer rifle. The shark responded by swimming away, actually reversing the direction of the power winch, then pulled the winch right off the floorboard of the boat and into the water.

"Whitey wasn't done yet," Pool said. "He returned and bit the guy's propeller right off."

At last report, Hank had moved to the mountains, renamed his boat the *Mackinaw King*, and was fishing at Lake Tahoe.

Only rarely has anybody tried fishing for Great White sharks. Regardless, it is now illegal to do so. Hopefully, this will insure the species' survival. Great Whites have roamed the open ocean without fear since prehistoric times. The next time you gaze across the open waters of the Pacific, you can be assured that the Big Guy is out there, never sleeping, always on the hunt, searching for where he can get his next bite.

❖

In 1994, the California State Fish and Game Commission passed a law that prohibits sportfishing for Great White sharks.

Tom and the gang on the John Muir Trail, below Cathedral Peak in Yosemite

On The
JOHN MUIR
TRAIL

In the Footsteps of a Legend

❖

You can have a foothold in the sky with almost every step on California's John Muir Trail.

The trail starts at practically the tip-top of North America—Mount Whitney—takes you northward across a land of 12,000-foot passes and Ansel Adams vistas, and eventually leads you into nature's showpiece of the world, Yosemite Valley. John Muir called the Sierra Nevada "the Range of Light," and the trail that traverses it has become America's greatest hike, 211 miles in all. It is a land spiked by 13,000-foot granite spires, untouched sapphire lakes loaded with trout, and canyons that drop as if they were the edge of the earth.

The hike includes some of the highest and most rugged trails in America, at times buried under tons of snow and ice. To reach the summit of Mount Whitney, the highest point in the continental U.S. at 14,496 feet, the hike starts at the Whitney Portal trailhead at 8,361 feet and climbs more than 6,100 feet in just 10 miles to reach the peak. If this is the first leg of a week-long trek and you're hauling a 55-pound pack of supplies, you might be shouting for the ghost of John Muir to bring up an oxygen tank before you're done.

The rewards, however, are unique and many. You find yourself in true high mountain wilderness where people are few, and deer and bears walk with little fear. The only sounds are the whistling birds, the rush of mountain streams, and enthusiastic whoops from your hiking companions as they view the panorama. After a week or so, many hikers say they start to feel purified by the high country.

The mountain range is speckled by thousands of lakes, most of them rock bowls carved by glacial action, then filled with water from snowmelt. This is the home of the golden trout, which are found only above 8,000 feet, with many of the lakes literally filled with them.

The excitement is tinged with a touch of danger. It's dangerous because thunderstorms that can rattle your brain are common in the high Sierra, and the bare, rocky passes far above tree line act as natural lightning rods. In rare instances, hikers are harpooned. It's dangerous because a slip in an icy pass can cause a fall of hundreds of feet. If you plan to climb Yosemite's Half Dome, the ascent is like walking up the side of San Francisco's Transamerica Pyramid building, holding onto a cable, your boots pressed against the granite wall.

But the beauty overshadows any fears. The rush of unbridled streams is the mountain anthem of the Sierra Nevada. Crystal-pure water is the lifeblood of the mountains, and here can be found the headwaters of some of California's mightiest rivers. The San Joaquin, the Kern, the Kings…they all start as trickles from the drips of melting snow.

Every step of the way, you are walking in the footsteps of legends: Muir, Carson, Walker… John Muir's first visit to the Sierra was in 1868 at the age of 30, and in the 45 years that followed, he became recognized as America's pioneer geologist for his hypothesis that glacial action led to the creation of Yosemite Valley and much of the Sierra Nevada. But though the mountains were Muir's classroom, they were also his church and sanctuary. It is for his love of the outdoors, and this region in particular, that he is best remembered.

"You cannot feel yourself out of doors; plain, sky and mountains ray beauty which you feel," Muir wrote. "You bathe in these spirit beams, turning around and round, as if warming at a campfire. Presently you lose consciousness of your own separate existence: You blend with the landscape, and become part and parcel of nature."

The Mount Whitney ridgeline looks like a row of giant wolf's teeth jutting into the sky. To hikers, the image may seem appropriate—this is one mountain that can chew you up.

From a distance, sheer rock outcrops give Whitney the appearance that it was sculpted by an angry giant with a hammer and chisel. If you feel like you're looking at the top of the world, it's because you are, or darn close. At 14,496 feet, the Whitney summit is the highest point in the Continental U.S. The peak of Mount Whitney marks the southern trailhead of the John Muir Trail, the greatest hike in the world, and that's why I was hiking it. Given three weeks, proper planning and a body in good condition, so can you.

Beyond the adventure itself, however, there is another element in the High Sierra that can seem eerie at times: You get the sensation that you're walking in the footsteps of John Muir, that somehow, Muir's ghost is with you, casting a shadow on the trail. "Walk away quietly in any direction and taste the freedom of the mountain," Muir said. "Climb the mountains and get their good tidings. Nature's peace will flow into you as sunshine flows into trees. The winds will blow their own freshness into you, and the storms their energies, while cares will drop off like autumn leaves."

But this freedom does not come without a price. And we sensed the reality of that price as we bulldogged our way toward Mount Whitney. At 12,000 feet, we approached a massive side of granite rock in which a narrow trail had been carved. "I feel like I'm on the moon doing a space walk, with one exception—gravity," said my brother, Rambob, an expedition member. Later, during a rest stop, he propped his pack up on a rock and looked at it as if it was full of lead, not food. "In one day, I've taught you to sit without falling down," he said to the pack. "Very good. Tomorrow, you're gonna learn how to walk."

This is one of the steepest hiking trails you can find anywhere. Some 100 switchbacks climb Wotan's Throne as you head up the big rock. Your pace is slow, each step as small as inches, with a deep breath per step. The air is thin up here in the high country; try to breathe too deep and you can cough your lungs out. After all, this is your first day on the trail and it takes at least three or four days to get acclimated to the altitude and the hike's physical demands.

A snowfield covered Wotan's Throne en route to Trail Crest, and we worked our way slowly across it, climbing as we went…11,000 feet, 12,000 feet, 13,000 feet… Looking to our left, we saw the rock mountain go straight up about 1,000 feet. Looking to our right, just three or four feet out, the mountain wall plunged 2,000 feet down into a snowfield. We were out there on the edge, and as safecrackers say, there were no false moves from there on out.

After the long crossing of the huge snowfield, we grappled our way across some boulders to gain a perch at Trail Crest at 13,560 feet. My engine was heating up, so I put a handful of snow under my hat to make a natural radiator. The Whitney summit beckoned, just two miles ahead. From the west side of Whitney, the ridgeline looks like millions of jagged-edged boulders piled atop each other to make a pyramid. The slog forward takes you within 400 feet of the top of Mount Muir.

In the final miles of the route to the Whitney summit, the ridge is cut by huge notch windows in the rock. You look through and the bottom drops thousands of feet, right at your boot tips. You're standing close to 14,000 feet in elevation, and to the east, you can see the town of Lone Pine at 3,800 feet, just 15 miles away.

The trail is as faint as the thin air, often blocked by snow, and marked by little piles of rocks placed by hikers along the way. With one last push, our small steps lifted us to the peak. I took a seat on a rock, wishing I had a 360-degree swivel on my neck. To the west was the entire Great Western Divide and much of Sequoia National Forest. To the east was the Owens Valley, almost 11,000 feet below. And to the north were rows of mountain peaks lined up for miles to the horizon—and somewhere among them was the path we would take to cross them. Ahead of us were 10 mountain passes, almost all of them at 11,000 to 12,000-foot elevations. We'd made it to the official start of the John Muir Trail.

Wrote Muir: "When looking for the first time from an all-embracing standpoint like this, the observer is oppressed by the incomprehensible grandeur, variety and abundance of the mountains rising shoulder to shoulder beyond the reach of vision; and it is only after they have been studied one by one, long and lovingly, that their far-reaching harmonies become manifest."

That night we camped below the Whitney Summit near Guitar Lake. It was a cold, clear sky, and when a full moon rose, it cast a pale hue, the color of Moby Dick, on the face of Whitney.

And in a way, the spirit of John Muir which permeates this trek is as elusive and ever-present as the great white whale itself.

One slip and tumble while climbing the trail to Forester Pass and you die. At 13,200 feet, this is the highest pass on the John Muir Trail. It is surrounded by miles and miles of barren crags, icebowl lakes and large snowfields. You glance at the mountain, a bare slab of granite wall covered by snow and ice, and you wonder, "How can a trail possibly climb this?"

You take out your binoculars and have a hard look. What you see, you don't like. The trail is literally cut into the wall—that is, what you can see of it, at times no more than three or four feet wide. After winter's snow, the trail crosses an ice-filled rock crevice that sits on the precipice of a 1,000-foot plunge. A slip here and you're gone. Some hikers use ice axes and crampons for safety at

Forester Pass. To keep our pack weight down, however, we left ours at home. When I saw the ice wall, I would have gladly made the trade. Without an ice ax, I didn't like the prospects.

None of us were yet acclimated to the altitude, now approaching 13,000 feet. I felt like my head was embedded with an ax. Expedition members Bob Stienstra, Jr., and Jeff Patty also had headaches, and Patty got a light nosebleed.

Mountain sickness can be an unpredictable and formidable opponent. It often strikes hikers who make rapid ascents of more than 8,000 feet, where thin air can affect the amount of oxygen that reaches your brain. It often starts with a fast pulse rate and a headache, similar to a hangover. In rare cases, if victims do not rest or descend to lower elevations, mountain sickness can evolve into what is called "high altitude pulmonary edema"—which brings with it fluid in the lungs, hallucinations and, shortly thereafter, probable death.

"Young, strong climbers seem particularly susceptible," said Jan Carline, a doctor who specializes in mountaineering ailments. "The healthy, well-conditioned climber is as frequently affected as the out-of-shape climber." If struck by the illness , the keys to recovery are resting, drinking water (dehydration is likely a partial cause) and making a descent to lower elevations, according to Carline.

"What's the plan?" said Patty, looking ahead to Forester Pass, the ascent of which lay just a mile or two away.

It was 3 p.m. and we had just seven miles of trail behind us for the day, about 30 for the trip. We needed to average about 12 miles per day in order to make trail's end before our backpack food ran out. That meant that any time we cut a day short, we would be forced into a longer day later. Three hours more on the trail would have likely solved Forester Pass. But ambition can be deadly in the High Sierra. Wisdom won out. After a close examination of Forester, we voted to stop.

"We camp here now and it gives our bodies 16, 17 hours before tomorrow morning to get better acclimated to the altitude," said

Patty. "When we tackle Forester in the morning, we'll not only be fresh, but our oxygen saturation level in our blood will be higher. We go up now and it could be a killer."

Rambob, at first ready to tackle the pass, later agreed with the decision. "Trail experience has nothing to do with intelligence," he said later. "It has to do with learning your lessons."

Over the years, we'd all been taught a few lessons in the mountains. And one of the best you can remember on the trail is to come to rational, group decisions, especially when dealing with the first symptoms of mountain sickness.

So we camped at Ice Lake, set at the foot of Forester Pass. We explored the area and found the high plateau country near Tawney Point is flooded with acres of wildflowers. Most of them are violet-colored lupine, their stalks bending to a light wind. Spring comes late in the high country. Even with Forester Pass looming ahead, such a sight causes a sudden calm to sweep over you. There's nobody up here in the high country today; just you, your companions, and miles of flowers and trail. You seem remarkably content with the present. John Muir called wildflower blooms like these "bee pastures" and wrote, "When California was wild, it was one sweet bee garden throughout its entire length, north and south, and all the way across from the snowy Sierra to the ocean."

The next morning, fresh and eager, Forester Pass snapped us back to the reality of the moment. Far above the treeline, there's not much except the narrow, rocky trail winding its way up the mountain, passing through sloping ice fields. Even after just a few slow steps on the ascent, I began to breathe in a rhythmic cadence as if I were running a marathon—steep trail, high altitude. The ice field at Forester can be a stopper. Its slope makes it a formidable crossing, and in the morning, when temperatures are still cold, its surface is slick and hard. I kept remembering my ice ax back at home. Walking across snowfields are one matter, where your boots sink a bit to make footholds, but ice demands a delicate touch. And don't look down here; a 2,000-foot drop can make you tipsy.

Slowly, with the caution of surgeons, we worked our way across the short, iced slope. Each step came after careful thought of where it would be placed. After two hours, we were safe, although maybe not completely sane. We were on top, at 13,200 feet, the highest pass on the John Muir Trail.

At the end of a long, gentle waterfall, I dunked my feet into a small pool, the cold, foaming water the best treatment available for a suddenly aching ankle. I was gazing at the Citadel, a towering peak that watches over the Kern River, when bang!—there was a sudden jolt at the heel of my right foot.

I pulled my foot out of the water, and incredibly, a trout had bitten it.

"I can just hear that trout at dinner time with his family," said my brother Bob, sitting alongside, eyebrows raised. "He'll say, 'Well, today I almost got me an outdoors writer.'"

It's true that the trout sometimes bite on almost anything, even feet, in the High Sierra, where the John Muir Trail leads to hundreds of small lakes and more than a dozen pristine streams loaded with trout. At Rae Lakes, both Rambob and I caught limits in 20 minutes using a bare hook for bait—and the only problem was the fish kept hitting the splitshot sinker instead of the hook.

The High Sierra is home for an abundance of fish and wildlife. Deer browse with little fear of man, black bear keep an eye out for your food, and little critters such as marmot, squirrels and chipmunks are your daily companions. It is the golden trout, however, that entices anglers to pack miles over mountain passes to reach prime fishing areas. This is California's state fish, a rare species that lives only above 8,000 feet; it's the most beautiful of all trout—a crimson stripe and many dark discs in a line along the side, a bright gold along the belly, with the top of its body lightly spotted. Rainbow, brown and brook trout are also abundant throughout the range. Many lakes, particularly in the southern Sierra from Lone Pine to Bishop, are stocked by the Department of Fish and Game from specially-equipped airplanes. But it is the golden trout, not the Fish and Game dink planters, that provide the most excitement and satisfaction.

At Mirror Lake, where hundreds of trout were rising to an insect hatch, we took a short hiking break and assembled our fishing rods. On my third cast, as I was looking at awesome Thor Peak, a trout ripped into my offering, a fly patterned after a caddis. Gulp. After a short tussle, I banked the fish, took a good look at it, then unhooked and released it. It was a rare, native golden trout. We decided to keep the more abundant brook and rainbow trout for dinner, the ultimate supplement to our small, freeze-dried backpackers' dinners. The trout bonus was coming nightly.

At Rae Lakes, tucked away just north of Glenn Pass (11,978 feet), the brook trout can swarm like anchovies in the sea, and there are periods where they hit anything you cast. In 90 minutes, my brother and I caught and released 150 to 200 trout between us. Despite the remoteness of the lakes, the park service limits camping there to one night only. Rangers do not want the natural beauty of the area trampled by high numbers of eager fishermen. But that is never really a problem, because the Sierra is loaded with many prime fishing areas.

You find bubbling, crystal-pure mountain streams filled with hungry native trout. In the evening, the trout often go on a feed that can have you catching and releasing them on many consecutive casts—before you move on to the next hole for more of the same. Rush Creek, hidden just south of Donahue Pass, a southeast border of Yosemite, is my personal favorite on the John Muir Trail. Though the lower stretches of Rush Creek have been drained dry in many years by L.A. Water and Power, the headwaters above Waugh Lake run fast and unbridled, with just enough holes, logs and pools to make homes for a bonanza fishery.

Some of the other top trout streams in the area include Lyell

Fork on the upper end of Tuolumne Meadows in Yosemite, the
Middle Fork of the Kings River, San Joaquin River below Evolution
Valley and Mono Creek below Bear Ridge.

The streams offer a challenge to anglers; you need careful
approaches followed by short, precise casts. You want things easy,
you say? Then just pick out a lake, where the trout practically say
"Catch me" every evening. The high mountain scenery is astound-
ing, and you might find yourself gazing off at a ridgeline—only to
be jolted back to the problem at hand with a fish on the line. With
the number of productive lakes, it's a take-your-pick situation. Our
favorites (south to north) include Bullfrog Lake near the Kearsage
Pinnacles, Rae Lakes, Lake Marjorie below Pinchot Pass (12,130
feet), and Marie Lake below Selden Pass (10,900 feet).

The prime areas can be reached only by foot or by horseback,
the same way John Muir explored these mountains more than 100
years ago. As a result, in many cases you can have a different stream
or lake to yourself each evening; just you, your rod and trout on the
bite. Just don't dangle your feet in the water too long.

We rounded a bend and came upon a hiker, crawling on his
hands and knees. He reached a boulder, then fell against it like a
discarded sack of dead fish. His eyes glazed over; he squinted at his
companions, unable to recognize them. He tried to talk, but the
words came out as incoherent babble.

"We need a rescue, quick," said Jim McDermond, a friend of the
ill man. "We're at 11,500 feet. We've got to get him to lower elevations or he's in big trouble."

All the symptoms pointed to the most severe form of "mountain
sickness," high altitude pulmonary edema. If the victim is not taken
to lower elevations, where the air is thicker, he will lapse into a
coma, and face death in six to 12 hours.

McDermond looked back at the trail, a faint path that cut

through rocky, craggy mountains for miles, far above the tree line. No shade, no doctors and no way to carry a hiker far in this rugged country. "There's a wilderness ranger station seven miles away," said McDermond. "It's all downhill from here. Without my pack, I think I can make it in a couple of hours and get help." He didn't wait for an answer. McDermond filled his canteen and ripped down the hill. He was out of sight in minutes. We waited behind.

This was at Helen Lake en route to Muir Pass. Of all the Sierra passes, it is the most aptly named. Just as John Muir was unlike any of his compatriots of 100 years ago, this pass is far different from any others in the High Sierra. Stark and cold for miles, it stands alone. No trees are in sight; just rocks, a faint trail that occasionally disappears under snow, lakes darkened from black glacial melt, and a flower here and there. The hike is long and high, a nine-mile climb with a vertical ascent of 4,000 feet—deep canyons and deep breaths.

At 11,000 feet, the trail borders the headwaters of the Middle Fork of the Kings River, where roaring whitewater tumbles down granite chutes. From Whitney Portal, we walked 90 miles to get there, and covering that much ground, the four of us began gaining a new perspective on the wilderness, a sense of a one-to-one relationship with the earth beneath our steps.

This was particularly true for Michael Furniss, a natural scientist who specializes in soil and water, who was explaining many of John Muir's findings on the creation of the Sierra Nevada.

"It was essentially flat land," Furniss said. "But through the forces of the earth's crust moving around, a large plate of granite was slowly lifted up, which gave rise to the very gentle western slope of the Sierra, and the abrupt cliff-like eastern slope. That cliff is the edge of the granite block or plate that rose up. The reddish rock on the ridgetops is the rock that was here before the Sierra rose up—it's more than a 100 million years old."

On the north side of Muir Pass, the dropoff into Evolution Valley is the Muir Trail's hidden jewel. Yet at one time, this lush country was as barren and lonely as Muir Pass, Furniss explained. Nature often behaves like a balance, and once it starts tipping, it continues in that direction for thousands of years. "What was once just a barren rock with a bit of lichen on it can develop into a forest," Furniss said. "How it works shows the true power of the wild. When even a small bit of vegetation gets a foothold in the desolate High Sierra, it holds soil and softens the winds. Over time, that allows more soil to accumulate and bigger plants to grow. Eventually, it can support a large and diverse plant system." It is an underlying principle of nature—that "everything is kind of hitched to everything else," as John Muir said.

The ill hiker lay on his side, still conscious. Words of comfort and assurance that "help is on the way" were offered, but the man neither recognized his companions nor was he able to decipher the simple words. When he coughed, you could hear the fluid building up in his lungs, a critical signal of the later stages of pulmonary edema. A tragedy seemed in the making.

But suddenly, off in the distance, a strange, faint sound filled the canyon. From miles away, it looked no larger than a black bug, and as it approached, the sound of blades whipping the air grew. It was a rescue helicopter.

In only a minute, the chopper landed, boarded the ill man and was off again, departing for lower elevations and professional medical aid. The rescue seemed a miracle. Maybe it was, but it was also an example of the work of the National Park Service.

When McDermond reached the wilderness ranger station, help was immediately summoned by George Durkee of the Park Service via the high-powered radio provided to all backcountry rangers. A rescue helicopter was dispatched immediately. In one month alone in Kings Canyon National Park, there were 60 such rescues, including four on the day McDermond's friend was retrieved.

We continued on, knowing the park service had saved a life. But with each step, I noticed the pain in my right ankle was getting sharper. I tried to ignore it.

In a sparse granite cavern of the High Sierra, droplets of snow-melt form the first little trickles of the San Joaquin River, just a few inches deep, 25 feet across. This is the start of one of America's most far-reaching river systems.

Furniss leaned down and dipped his Sierra Cup in the stream, then took a long draw of the cool water. "It doesn't come any better than this," he said with a grin.

Up here at 11,320 feet with not a tree in sight, it's difficult to imagine this is the same river that has set off health warnings for an area hundreds of river miles away from here, way down in the Central Valley, where pesticides washed from farmers' fields and irrigation diversions have turned the San Joaquin into a toxic sewer.

In the high country, far from the reach of industrial development, life is still pure, and so are the rivers that provide the lifeblood for California.

"The water that drains from the High Sierra is some of the highest quality in the world," Furniss said. "It is extremely soft, very low in sediment, and very clear and cold. Because it is so soft, it carries very little nutrient value. Algae growth is very low." The lack of algae results in a bonus for Sierra hikers because stream rocks are so clean that your steps can be firm and certain, rather than the slip-and-slide so common when crossing lower elevation streams.

There are thousands of miles of waterways in the Sierra Nevada, and most of them tumble their way down granite canyons. They occasionally charge down waterfalls into pools foaming with oxygen bubbles. But in upper Yosemite is Lyell Fork, one of the more unique streams in the High Sierra range. Instead of rumbling over boulders, the current barely moves. It meanders through the upper end of Tuolumne Meadows, this way and that. "Most all rivers in all places form their own canyons," Furniss said. "River canyons of the Sierra have been carved out by enormous masses of moving ice—glaciers. The rivers are set in awesome, deep canyons."

The first indication of the abundant chain of life these streams provide came on the first day of the expedition. We forded Lone Pine Creek, just 10 feet wide and two feet deep, and at a log crossing, when my feet hit the log, several trout darted out beneath my steps. It was a sign. From little critters such as squirrels and marmots to big fellows like bears, these creeks provide water fountains for all wildlife. Hikers benefit the same.

Most of the rivers in the southern range drain into the San Joaquin, to the Sacramento Delta, and ultimately, out through San Francisco Bay.

When the snow melts, the tiny drops of water slide off rocks and join in crevices and small pools. When they overflow, gravity takes the water down into fissures. Eventually, the chain continues until the headwaters of a major river have been formed. Gurgling creeks, polished stones, wild trout rising to a stonefly. It is the rivers that make the mountains come alive.

John Muir called the rush of High Sierra streams "the mountain symphony," and backpackers develop an ear for this music. At night, when I roll out my sleeping bag, I always find myself laying it parallel to the river, my head on the upstream side. As I look at the stars, it somehow feels like the river is flowing through me, quieting my mind, yet filling me with energy for the next day's miles of trail.

Giant thunder rolls rattled off the canyon rim and tumbled down the valley. We looked up into the black clouds and watched lightning bolts ricochet off mountain tops.

Almost all of the sparse lodgepole pines at 10,000 feet have been fried at one time or another by lightning bolts. Backpackers can get the same treatment if they find themselves on a barren rock ridge when a thunderstorm suddenly moves in. Hiking is seldom considered a dangerous sport, but more backpackers are struck by lightning than scuba divers are munched by sharks.

Massive black clouds were forming above and thunderclaps were ripping along the mountain tops. With a barren mountain pass a mile ahead, we had no place to hide.

The Minarets ridgeline over Garnet Lake looks like a monument, and in a way it is—to Ansel Adams. It was one of his favorite places to photograph. As a tribute, the area is now named the Ansel Adams Wilderness. It was one of John Muir's hideaways as well. The ridge is topped by Mount Ritter at 13,300 feet, first climbed by John Muir in 1872. It is "the king of the mountains of the middle portion of the Sierra," he said. The Minarets provide a series of some of the most spectacular vistas on the John Muir Trail. To reach it, we crossed nine mountain passes and over 195 miles of trail, including sidetrips, since our start at Whitney Portal near the town of Lone Pine. Yosemite awaited over the next pass—Donahue Pass at 11,056 feet.

But hikers rarely feel like rushing away from the Ansel Adams Wilderness. My pace had been slowed by an ankle injury. Each day my right ankle swelled larger, and despite being bandaged, taped and soaked, there were times when each step felt like an ice pick being jabbed and torqued. The long climbs were not so difficult, but the steeps descents were killers. At times, I used a hiking stick like a crutch. About five times, with a sudden jab of pain, the ankle collapsed under my weight, and I went careening down into rocks. But I couldn't quit. With the ghost of Muir looming overhead, I felt as if we were on a mission. Besides, what better place to just stop and gaze at the surroundings? Below the Minarets, the lakes looked like a series of mountain jewels. Shadow Lake and Thousand Island Lake were particular favorites of John Muir, and within 10 miles was the geologic phenomenon of Devil's Postpile.

Even after walking almost 200 miles, the beauty of Shadow Lake still snaps your head to attention. It is tucked away below the Minarets, with shadows of the surrounding peaks and high mountain rims reflected on the water. Early morning sunlight and light breezes send silver ripples across the surface. The lake seems to have a personality, a depth to it, something you feel rather than see. Few lakes anywhere have this presence—Crater Lake in Oregon is one of the few others that does.

"I first discovered this charming lake in the autumn of 1872, while on my way to the glaciers at the head of the river," wrote John Muir. "It was rejoicing then in its gayest colors, untrodden, hidden in the glorious wildness like unmined gold." In order to keep it this way, no camping is permitted at Shadow Lake. Nearby Rosalie Lake, Garnet Lake and Thousand Island Lake provide similar spectacular settings below the Minarets, but with less fragile surroundings.

It was at Shadow Lake where we met a team of hikers sweating out a climb, when they stopped to catch their breath.

"We're going to the Evil Postpile," said one. Where? "The Evil Postpile."

They showed me their map. It had been creased in such a way that the "D" in "Devil" could not be read. Well, the Postpile is anything but evil, and far from the creation of the Devil as well.

It is the best example in the world of what geologists call "columnar jointed rock," where near-perfect rock columns rise 60 feet tall. Their fragility is such that a huge pile of boulders sits in front of the postpile—actually broken pillars from years of erosion and earthquakes. Its creation started about 100,000 years ago, quite recently according to geologic time, as a result of the cooling of basalt lava. In contrast, the mountains surrounding Devil's Postpile are millions of years old.

Up in the Minarets, to the west, Mount Ritter was being bombarded by lightning bolts. To the east, the Sierra Crest was reining in more thunderheads. We were on the craggy trail between the two, climbing to the pass, shaking off raindrops and praying the lightning bolts would not find us. There was a silent tension among us. Furniss stopped in his tracks and raised his hands up toward the clouds. "I'm ready, Lord," he said. "Take me." But at least for this moment, no lightning bolt was forthcoming. Patty frowned, then announced, "Hey, I'm 6-foot-5. I don't like the odds."

Afternoon thundershowers are common in the high country, especially on hot summer days. The 10- to 15-mile canyons that sit between the mountain passes create their own little worlds, and each seems to attract its own weather system. Earlier on the trip, while fishing in sunlight one afternoon at Marjorie Lake, just a few miles above us beyond Pinchot Pass there was an awesome thunder and lightning storm. We missed it that time, and we were hoping for the same good luck at Island Pass—but it sounded like the gods were having a game of bowling in the clouds directly above us.

Suddenly, I felt a light wind coming up the canyon from behind. Furniss immediately stopped in his tracks. Simultaneously, we looked at the rain clouds and Mount Ritter.

"Those clouds are moving out," Furniss said. "That wind is blowing them into the next canyon. It looks like we'll be okay."

With a quick stroke of nature's magic, we were steered clear from danger. In an hour, we were safely at the top, map in hand, gazing at the next peak, just five miles away.

"That's Donahue Pass," Patty said. "Yosemite is just on the other side. When we get there and drop down into the valley, Half Dome will be waiting for us. The climb is almost straight up, and we'll use cables to hold on to."

My limp was getting so pronounced that nearly every passing hiker stopped to ask for an explanation.

One last push and puff up the trail and we scaled the top of Donahue Pass at 11,056 feet, the last of the high mountain crosses on the John Muir Trail.

Donahue is a southeastern border to Yosemite Park, and we sat on our rock perch for a lunch of jerky, nuts and dried fruit, gazing down at the head of Tuolumne Meadows 2,000 feet below. Tranquility was setting in among the four of us, knowing a 7,000-foot descent was ahead over the final 35 miles. Suddenly, a tremendous roar in the distance spiked our bubble.

It sounded like a giant thunderclap, and we all jerked our heads toward Mount Lyell to the south, the source of the explosion. We saw a gigantic landslide reshaping a thousand feet of the mountain's slope. You may see the power of these mountains unleashed in only seconds, but you will remember it for years.

Another element of power that you see on the John Muir Trail is the resilience of people on the trail, old and young, male and female alike. Day after day, people show the capacity to reach within for that little something extra, and find it.

We learned this early. On the second day of the trip, on the backside of Mount Whitney, we ran into a pair of old-timers who gave the appearance of long miles and trail savvy.

"Where you headed?" I asked.

"Tuolumne Meadows," said Burton Lenker, 65, from Lynchburg, Virginia. "The way we got it figured, we only got about 200 miles to go with 600 behind us. We started at the Mexico border. I guess I'd never do it again; down South, you got 20 miles between water and nothing but scrub brush and hot ground."

"Why do you do it?"

"Have to," he answered.

People come from all over America to hike the John Muir Trail, or at least portions of it. Jim Penkusky and Susan Day of Columbia, Maryland, started north from the Mexico border on the Pacific Crest Trail, part of which connects with the John Muir Trail, and hoped to reach Canada by mid-October. We connected with them at little Gladys Lake north of Reds Meadow.

"The rangers in northern Washington said they usually get their first big snow before or after the first week of November," Penkusky said. "We're aiming to finish a little ahead of that. That's when the weather window shuts down."

"Why do you do it?"

"I feel like I've been called to these mountains for years."

By foot or by horse, the mountains do seem to call for you. Dick

Greve of New Jersey is a junior high school teacher, and spends each summer tromping across America's wildlands. We met him surveying the view from 12,100-foot Mather Pass. His pack was covered with patches, including one that says "2,000-miler"—for completing the 2,140-mile Appalachian Trail, from Georgia to Maine.

"Most people that try the AT (Appalachian Trail) will be out in California the next year for the JMT (John Muir Trail)," said Greve. "This is the highest hiking trail in the world. The High Sierra is utterly spectacular, especially for a guy used to the East Coast like myself."

Many hikers who make the entire trip from Mount Whitney to Yosemite are high school teachers and professors. As educators, they have the spare time in the summer—three weeks is about right for the trail. Finding the time is a major problem for most. Mike Little of Columbiana, Ohio, is a good example.

"I teach geology and biology at Boardman High School," Little said when we met along the San Joaquin River. "I first came out here as a matter of curiosity, and to gather information for my students. But after hiking about a hundred miles, the country here has been like a magnet. I had to come back this summer so I could finish up the entire John Muir Trail."

If hikers don't have the time, energy or equipment to complete the entire trail, an advantage is that it crosses through three national parks and two wilderness areas managed by the U.S. Forest Service. As a result, several cross-trails bisect the trail. This allows hikers to design shorter loop trips, yet still connect to a section of the John Muir Trail. That is exactly what most Californians do, making the most of a long weekend or a week of vacation.

But a strange phenomenon seems to envelop hikers who are in the backcountry for a short time. In typical conversations, they will top whatever adventure you describe, as if it is a contest.

"How was the snow at Muir Pass?" asked one hiker.

"Not bad," answered Rambob. "We had to cross a few small glaciers and snowfields, but that was it."

"You guys had it easy," said the hiker. "When I did it in '82, I had seven miles of snow crossing. It was rough, but I made it."

Many meetings with hikers go just like this. "In '78, I went up the Golden Staircase in 100-degree weather," said one hiker. "The next day it snowed nine inches on me when I was climbing Mather Pass. It was much tougher than what you guys have got on this trip."

Finally, my brother came up with a response.

"Well, we decided to take it easy this time around," my brother answered. "Back in '82, we did the entire John Muir Trail backwards on a pogo stick."

What you discover is that the longer you stay in the mountains, the less important seems the merit of your feats. What develops instead is a feeling of oneness with your surroundings. Eventually, this bonds all hikers.

"Most people are on the world, not in it," wrote John Muir. "(They) have no conscious sympathy or relationship to anything about them—undiffused, separate, and rigidly alone like marbles of polished stone, touching but separate. (But) when one is alone at night in the depths of these woods…Every leaf seems to speak… Perfect quietude is there, and freedom from every curable care."

From the perch of a rock cornice atop Half Dome, Yosemite Valley below seems one of the world's true miracles.

You try a nervous seat on Half Dome's overhang, your legs dangling over the edge, and feel the mercurial sensation that comes with a one-in-a-million experience. Below is nearly a mile of empty air, yet you are encircled by perhaps the most magnificent landscaping on earth. The valley is framed by El Capitan, the Goliath of Yosemite, on one side, and three-spired Cathedral Rocks on the other. To the northeast is glacial-carved Tenaya Canyon, still a wild, untamed land, trailless and forbidding. Low-hanging cumulus thunderheads cover the sky from rim to rim, what hikers call "Ansel Adams clouds." The canyon walls, massive exposures of granite, are crossed by long, silver-tasseled waterfalls.

To reach this perch, we walked, crawled and clawed 240 miles including sidetrips, from the summit of Mount Whitney to Yosemite Valley. In the High Sierra, we discovered the people few and friendly, the fish and wildlife many and spirited. Each evening's camp was pitched in virtual solitude, a trout dinner in the pan, with frequent visits from marmot, squirrels and deer. On the final day, Yosemite crowned it, especially from the top of Half Dome.

Some Californians, especially those who have never left blacktop pavement, consider Yosemite a place to avoid. It's a city in the mountains, they say, with too many people and too little space. But beyond the overpeopled valley—primarily congested at the tourist stores and restaurant areas—the lonely splendors still await those willing to hike to them. Yosemite contains some 1,200 square miles and 90 percent of it is roadless wilderness. There may be no more spectacular and popular a climb than to the top of Half Dome, which juts almost straight up from the valley. The last 500 feet of the ascent is up a granite face that is nearly perpendicular, where the "hike" becomes more like an act of faith. You grab onto a steel cable, then press booted feet against the granite wall and pull your way up, step by step.

Most people fix their attention on their every move, never taking their eyes from each step and handhold. After 20 minutes of this, I figured I must be near the top and innocently glanced down—and instead found myself smack in the middle of the rock facing, the valley floor plunging thousands of feet below. I felt a bit dizzy, but steadied myself with the cable, then looked down again.

John Muir was the ninth person ever to reach the top of Half Dome, doing so in the fall of 1875 at the age of 37, using the rope left in place from the first climb made a few months earlier by George Anderson. "The first view was perfectly glorious," wrote Muir. "A massive cloud of pure pearl lust, apparently as fixed and calm as the meadows and groves in the shadow beneath it, was arched across the valley from wall to wall, one end resting on the grand abutment of El Capitan, the other on Cathedral Rock." Many present-day hikers have stood in the same spot where Muir made that observation. The cable makes it possible.

The park was named after the Ahwahneechee Indian tribe, which first inhabited the valley. Their name for grizzly bear was *Uzumati*, and when the tribe fought deportation to a reservation, their fierce resistance gained them the Indian name for the grizzly. But *U-zu-ma-ti* somehow came out "Yosemite." The first white man to see Yosemite Valley was Joe Walker in 1833, the trailblazer who didn't follow trails, but made them. Walker may have been the greatest of all Western explorers, but his tombstone simply reads "Camped in Yosemite, November 12, 1833."

At the foot of Vernal Falls, just a mile from the end of our trip, I wondered how many times Walker, and later John Muir, had stood at the same spot. I was listening to the rush of water here when a middle-aged couple approached me.

"Can we take a picture of you?" they asked. "You look like a hiker."

After a snapshot, the woman asked, "Did you really camp up in the mountains the whole night?"

"Up there," I pointed up the canyon, "and far beyond."

A mile down the trail, as we touched down into the valley floor at trail's end at Happy Isles, we were suddenly amid hundreds of tourists glued to their cars and blacktop. There was little talk of the trip home; we were already thinking that it was time to go back to the high country. By the time we reached our car, we were talking of our favorite places on the trail, places we would certainly return to.

The words of John Muir rang clear: "The mountains are calling, and I must go."

The next day, I reported to Dr. Fred Behling, an orthopedist at Stanford who specializes in sports injuries.

"You've got a broken ankle," he said, looking at the x-rays. "Worse, you've got pieces of bone floating around in there. We'll have to operate. But your ankle is so inflamed and swollen that we'll have to wait until it quiets down in there. Just how did you do this?"

"I just finished hiking 250 miles, from Mount Whitney to Yosemite Valley," I told him. "On the third day, coming down to Rae Lakes, I felt something pop."

He measured my calf muscle. My left calf was two inches larger than the right calf, apparently from the limp I had developed. Then Behling grinned.

"Two hundred fifty miles, eh?" he said with a wink. "Yeah, *of course...* It's physically impossible to walk with an ankle that looks like this. But don't worry, I won't tell anybody. You know, I read your fish report. I understand about you outdoors writers."

❖

To hike the entire John Muir Trail, you need wilderness permits for Mount Whitney, Kings Canyon and Yosemite. For Mount Whitney, phone (619) 876-5542. For Kings Canyon, phone (209) 565-3341. For Yosemite, phone (209) 372-0200. Yosemite provides wilderness permits on a quota system, half by mail in advance and half on a first-come, first-served basis.

You will also need Forest Service maps for Sierra National Forest, Sequoia National Forest and Inyo National Forest. These can be obtained by writing to Forest Service Office of Information, 630 Sansome Street, San Francisco, CA 94111. Phone (415) 705-2874.

Rafting the Klamath at flood stage—on the way to Hell's Corner

Klamath
CHALLENGE

1,000 Rapids at Flood Stage

❖

Rafting the Klamath River at flood stage can feel like being declared fish bait in a river full of piranhas.

The big rapids have names like Satan's Gate, Scarface and Devil's Toenail. They are bank-to-bank sheets of whitewater with hidden flip holes and vortexes. In an instant, you can find yourself popcorned out of your seat and into the river, tumbling downstream, wondering when you will have a chance for your next breath of air.

This is the Klamath River: In 200 miles, there are more than a thousand rapids. If you figure dumping your raft is a 1,000-to-1 long shot, that means your number is coming up.

We called our expedition the "Klamath Challenge" and it was the first documented attempt to run the entire Klamath River, from its savage headwaters in Oregon all the way to the Pacific Ocean on California's north coast. We were six men in three small rafts, running the river when streamflows were 6 to 10 times the velocity of summer flows, when rafting is most popular.

In late winter of 1986, a phenomenon occurred in which the northern jet stream dipped down into Northern California, and the southern jet stream suddenly rose into central California. The jet streams then meshed, creating monsoon-like rains across the Bay Area and Northern California. Many major rivers flooded, including the mighty Klamath, a massive course of cold, muddy water. For example, at Orleans, the river was running at 30,000 cubic feet per second (cfs); 2,000 to 3,000 cfs is its typical velocity. The opportunity to raft a river in such conditions only occurs a few times in a century.

The reality of that struck home after just 15 minutes on the water. We beached the 12-foot rafts, then hiked along the shoreline to scout a rapid called Caldera, which appeared to be nothing but whitewater and waves for 500 yards.

"It's called Caldera because it looks like a boiling cauldron," said Dean Munroe, our chief guide. It was running at 6,000 cubic feet per second, or six times its normal velocity.

We pushed off toward Caldera Rapid and when we hit the first river hole, the boat dropped 15 feet at a 45-degree angle. Everything went black. Later I figured out why—I had closed my eyes. I sensed ice-cold water everywhere. Am I in the raft or not? How long can I hold my breath?

It was just a few miles downriver from there, at a rapid called Ambush, where Munroe and two others once wrapped their rafts around a rock. A metal snap on a hook actually straightened, and the line attached to it came shooting back and struck Munroe in the face. He broke his nose and was blinded in his right eye.

Since that accident, Munroe has run thousands of miles of rivers. He is believed to be the first rafter to run the McCloud River, Hell's Corner Gorge on the Klamath, and Wooley Creek, a feeder stream to the Salmon River. He knows what it is like to be out on the edge, and he likes it there. He looked at Caldera Rapid like it was an old foe he knew well, but feared.

"When the boat hits a wave, the front will rise up and get pushed back," Munroe said. "It feels like you're hitting a rock. The paddler has to reach in front and bite into the water to pull the boat down. You've got to reach out and grab water like you're grabbing for a life insurance policy."

Beaver trappers in the 1800s asked the Indians the name of the great river, and they answered *Klamet* or *Tlamath*, which means "swiftness." Over the years, it has been adapted to Klamath. It is one of the West's great rivers, older than the mountains around it, and it remains one of California's last free-flowing, unbridled streams, running free for 187 miles from below Iron Gate Dam near the Oregon border.

The headwaters of the Klamath start in Oregon as just trickles from a series of streams, the Sycan, Williamson, and Lost rivers. Eventually the water bores through Klamath Canyon and, after being dammed at Copco and Iron Gate lakes, tumbles free in California. It cuts a path from sparse grasslands to canyons rimmed by conifer forests, and then through groves of Douglas firs and redwoods, the tallest trees in the world.

The river picks up velocity as it narrows, and gains volume with every feeder stream, the Shasta, Scott, Salmon and Trinity rivers. That combination of velocity and volume gives the river punch, the kind that can make rafting more an act of faith than a float trip.

Hell's Corner Gorge, a five-mile stretch in Oregon, is the Klamath's most scorching section. It has 15 major rapids, from Gunsmoke to Branding Iron to Bushwhacker, including many rated Class V. That's just one step below Class VI, which is considered suicide. But we had no plans to paddle the big river in the sky. We were wearing "dry suits," body-length waterproof suits with rubber seals at the neck, wrists and ankles. In addition, we were wearing the most buoyant life vests available. The two in combination worked to keep us mostly dry and floating.

Our guides, Dean Munroe of Redding, Bob Claypole of Klamath River and Greg Talamini of San Rafael, had more than 10,000 miles of river between them, giving them the know-how and the instincts to take care of the rough stuff. "If it gets too rough, we just go swimming," Munroe said. Photographer Kurt Rogers, myself and expedition member Rich Cottrell set out to oar 200 miles of river. We were using 12-foot, self-bailing rafts. The raft is called "self-bailing" because the floor inflates, and is tied to the sides of the raft so water can pass in and out without the paddlers having to bail. It bails the water out even quicker when it flips upside down.

From my perch at the front of the raft, I felt like a hood ornament on a car sailing off a cliff. The raft would crash down into a water hole, disappear under the river waves, then pop up 30 yards downstream.

I shook the water from my eyes and noticed I was still in the boat. My paddle had disappeared, so I just hung on as well as was possible.

"So this is Caldera," I thought. The first of a thousand rapids.

You had to time each breath as the raft cascaded through the big water. If there was too much water to see, you didn't breathe. We plowed through a big flip hole, and then a diagonal wave hit us from the right, raising up the side of the raft.

An instant later, another wave rammed us. It picked up the boat and dumped us out like a monster shaking a new bottle of ketchup. We were suddenly in the river, enveloped in a remarkable surge of cold, bubbling water.

There's no time to think or react; your body goes on automatic pilot. When I popped up, I was under the overturned raft with the sound of crashing water echoing inside it. I grabbed a quick breath of air. You don't think, you just do. I ducked down and swam around the boat, popped up and grabbed another breath. The river claws at you, pulls you under, then spits you out. An eddy was on our right, and my partner and I used its crosscurrents like a conveyer belt to take us to the shoreline.

We both looked upriver, and just like that, there was another raft upside down. Moments later, Rich Cottrell appeared near us, waist deep in the water, water gushing from him, a look of terror, shock and "I'm going to live after all" in his eyes.

"It happened so fast I only had time to get one yell out," Cottrell said. "We flipped and had to float through 600 yards of rapids, going up and down the chutes. I sucked some water."

His partner, Greg Talamini, emerged on the other side of the river with the overturned raft. The third raft, we later learned, was wrapped around a rock. The rafters were wet, cold and shook up, but nobody was hurt.

At camp that night, Munroe kicked the campfire and thought of the big water we had crossed, and what lay ahead. "Yes," he said, "Hell's Corner Gorge deserves its name. There's some serious stuff ahead and the worst of it is the Ikes. We'll be hitting those. I like making history, like to feel the hair raising up on my neck."

He kicked the fire again and little sparks went shooting into the night sky. They disappeared, like the dreams of those who have lost their lives on the Klamath.

A ghost named Ike might still be rafting the Klamath River rapids that bear his name.

The Ikes are a long series of 10-foot rollers, Grand Canyon-style rapids and waves, big water made even bigger by the flooding of the Klamath. They are Ike, Big Ike and Super Ike. In a raft, you head for each crest and try to punch through, disappearing under water for a few seconds, then plunging straight down into a deep river hole, the hydraulics of the suck hole yanking you and the raft under.

"We should be reaching the Ikes by midafternoon," said Claypole, looking at the map while I guided the boat, directing it with various oar strokes. "But to get there, we'll have to get past Savage, Mixmaster, the Trench and others." After a while, you begin to feel like you're in a submarine, not a raft.

When you're at the oars, the idea is to point the boat at the shoreline, keeping trouble spots directly in front of the raft. Then you can pull the oars back with all your might, rowing to stay away from rock outcrops, flip holes and vortexes that can haul you down and keep you there.

The river is like a motor on your boat, pushing you at 5 to 10 miles per hour, sometimes faster. But this motor never turns off, and that forces you to make snap decisions. The river does not wait for you. To keep a fresh man at the oars, we would trade every 30 minutes or so.

At one big rock, I tried to skirt the raft along the edge of a whirlpool, but it literally sucked us in and spun us around 180 degrees before spitting us downriver. At least we were still upright. "I better take over at the Ikes," Claypole said with a laugh.

Rafts that flip at the Ikes often go completely airborne at a 45-degree angle before turning over and dumping their occupants. To reach the Ikes, though, first we would have to pass through Ishi Pishi Falls.

Ishi Pishi is the Klamath's only Class VI rapid, where luck plays a larger role than skill in surviving it in a raft. Many ghosts roam its rocky foam. From the river canyon above, Ishi Pishi looks like it's half rapid, half waterfall. It is a 300-yard whiteout, spiked with house-sized boulders and 15-foot holes. Named by the Karok Indians, *Ishi Pishi* means end of the trail. They knew what they were talking about.

Over the years, many Karok dip netters have fallen here and drowned. The most recent deaths came in the mid-eighties when three Indians took a motorboat across the river just above Ishi Pishi in order to fish on the far side. The motor cut out, the boat was swept through the falls and flipped, and all three men died.

Only one team of rafters is known to have run Ishi Pishi and survived, although the boat flipped and there were several injuries and near-drownings. James Quinn of Oregon led a team of rafters in a 17-footer, a big river raft by any standards. Brad Throgmorton, a steelhead guide who lives just above Ishi Pishi, was offered a seat in the raft, but decided to watch instead.

"They hit a big suck hole, and the raft started to wallow," Throgmorton told me. "The oarsman jumped out of the boat, holding onto the railing, hoping to catch the current with his body to pull the boat out, but he was swept right out and the boat started to flip. Quinn's leg stuck between the bottom of the frame and the boat, and then it flipped upside down. With my binoculars, I felt like I was in the boat with them. I've done enough rafting so that I was living it blow-by-blow with them. My knees were actually trembling and I lost my breath."

It was a miracle that no one drowned, although Quinn came close. He came out of it with a broken hand and a warning for all rafters: Do not attempt it. At Ishi Pishi, we took his advice and portaged. Then it was on to the Ikes.

The raft rammed through the first cresting wave, and the Klamath was all around us. I shook my head clear of water. "Great, we're still in the raft," I thought. But just up ahead near the left bank, the raft with photographer Kurt Rogers was locked in a swirling eddy. In a flash, we skirted past him.

"It took three tries to get out," he said later. "The hydraulics had us locked in. There was almost nothing we could do."

Meanwhile, the third raft of our team started to flip when it hit a wave at an angle, and its occupants, Greg Talamini and Rich Cottrell, threw their bodies across the rubber boat in panic dives to weigh down the high side of the boat. That kept the raft down, but Cottrell almost fell out of the boat in the process.

Welcome to Ike, with more to come. You take a deep breath and bite your paddle into the waves. Water everywhere, so cold you get a headache. Maybe you suck a little down the pipes, too. One after another, the big waves come. The raft powers into them, disappears under water, then pops up 15 yards downstream. Still okay. No time to think. You time your breathing, taking a big gulp of air when you can find it. You're out there on the edge, working a high wire without a net. Big Ike has come and gone, and you're still floating.

Then Super Ike completely envelops the boat and you disappear, raft and all, under water, then finally pop up. Air never tasted so good before.

You're not aware of time, just of the whitewater ahead of you.

Then suddenly, we went around a bend and the river flattened.

Three little rafts were floating down the river at the bottom of giant slick canyon walls. A pair of mergansers flew by and looked at us, wondering what we were doing there. Maybe the ghost rafter Ike was wondering the same thing.

When you climb a mountain, you're in control of yourself. But when you run down the Klamath, you are being guided, the river in control. A greater force decides your fate.

All was quiet. As we floated downstream, the ocean only a few days away, we were surrounded by a fish and wildlife haven. The feeder streams to the Klamath River pour from a mountain knot that hides some of the most diverse country in America. On the river, which provides access for anybody, you can see a continual abundance of birds, wildlife and fish.

As you tumble and float down the river, you feel as if you are being allowed to view nature's secrets. The feeling comes quickly: At our put-in at Iron Gate Dam, a golden eagle winged past. Each mile brings something new, if you look for it.

In the first 100 miles, we saw 25 species of birds, as well as otters and deer. Claypole, who lives in a cabin about 40 yards from the river, told me he had seen 125 species of birds in a 10-year span. Scientists say there are 280 species of animals along the Klamath.

"This country is a coming together of different mountains," Claypole said. "It's ancient and diversified. That's why so many different kinds of birds and mammals live here. The river comes alive with birds, and we're like intruders getting a secret glimpse."

In the spring, the most abundant birds are nesting waterfowl, primarily mergansers, mallards and Canadian geese. Osprey, which nest on the top of dead trees, and blue heron cruise up and down the river canyon. Occasionally we saw turkey vultures staring at us from their perches, apparently waiting for us to tip over.

Rivers are the lifeblood of this world; without them, we have nothing. The fisheries on the Klamath are prime examples of that. The Klamath remains home to one of the largest steelhead runs anywhere, with fish arriving from the ocean from August to April.

When trailblazer Jedediah Smith first saw the Klamath, he said there were so many salmon that "you could walk across the river on their backs." Now special controls are needed in an attempt to resurrect this once-great fishery. Fifty years of overharvest from commercial fishing and Indian netting—as well as significant damage to spawning habitat from heavy logging—has reduced the once-great salmon population here.

As we made our way, we could see spring coming to the river in different stages. On the upper river, the plants were just starting to bud. Down at Happy Camp near the Ikes, the pines were inching out growth on every limb. Wildflowers were blooming, among them fawn lilies and red larkspur. No matter what the river might hold in store for us, the beauty along the riverbanks transcended all.

The sound of the surf was the payoff we'd been paddling for. We'd had several good dunkings, with 150 miles behind us and 50 miles to go. While the river was running high, cold and green, the rapids were now behind us. Ahead was Indian territory, the confluence of the Trinity River and the Pacific Ocean.

"That outgoing tide might pull us right out into the ocean," said Dean Munroe, the head guide. "But first we have to get that far. The spring winds out of the north could stop us dead in the water."

"What if the locals start throwing rocks at us from the top of the river canyon?" asked Bob Claypole at the oars, who had had that experience not long before while steelhead fishing.

"We just don't know what's going to happen," responded Munroe. "What we're doing hasn't been done before so we don't know what to expect. But I want to hear those ocean waves, and I want to touch down on a sandy beach."

The final leg of the trip had a set of new problems. Would coastal winds stop us? Would an incoming tide force us to camp in forbidden Indian territory? What if Indians objected to our crossing through their lands? We pushed toward the Hoopa Valley Indian Reservation, where Hupas live near the town of Weitchpec, and further downriver live the Yuroks.

As we paddled, I remembered the days I spent on the reservation with Jimmy Jackson, a Hupa tribal elder. I remember how the old Indian tugged on his hat and shrugged at my questions about the conflicts with the younger generation.

"Let me tell you about lies," Jackson said. "When somebody tells a lie, it goes and hides under a rock someplace. Pretty soon somebody is going to come along and pick that rock up and the lie comes out for everybody to see. That's what's happening to some of these younger fellers these days. Are they going to pay? You betcha they're going to pay."

The Klamath River has thousands of years of Indian legend, know-how and worship in its history. But in the past 25 years, that precious ancient knowledge, the stuff of woods and water, is coming apart and being lost like an old rope unraveling.

"These young fellers don't listen to us," said Jackson. "They don't even speak the language. They don't think, 'Maybe I've caught enough fish.' I learned everything from my parents and cousins, and they learned everything from theirs. It used to take us months to make a small net out of wild iris, and we'd stand on a rock and dip it to try and catch a fish. Now they go to the store and buy gillnets from the white man."

We were heading toward Indian territory. The oars of our raft dipped in the water, and with a push, the boat floated under the bridge at Weitchpec. All was quiet, except for the sound of water slipping by the raft. It was here in 1985, while I was standing on the bridge, that seven rifle shots went whistling by below me. Some of the younger Indians who lived here weren't too friendly to outsiders.

The violence was rare, but it did occur. The Indian culture was enduring an overhaul and the glitches in the transition rose to the surface. There was often a split between the older Indians who wanted to live with the land in peace, following the old traditions, and the younger tribe members, split between cultures, looking for a place to vent those feelings.

"The old Indians learned to live on the earth with cycles that we don't even recognize," said Claypole, pushing the oars while we floated down the river. "They knew what plants were good for medicine, and what you could eat, what you couldn't. The old Indians could live off the land. A lot of that is being lost."

The ancient Klamath has been cutting through these mountains for millions of years. It hasn't changed much. Only the people have changed, nature outliving man's frailty. Claypole looked up at the canyon walls while speaking. "There may yet come a day when we will need to reclaim the old Indians' knowledge."

We hit Indian territory at 10 a.m., floating past where the Trinity River pours into the Klamath. The Trinity, a big river, entered as a milky green, mixing with the darker Klamath. No one was in sight, not even at the Weitchpec store, a local hangout.

The river pushed us on, now just 40 miles from the coast, a light wind in our faces. We waved at two Indians on a sandbar as we passed. Everyone was friendly and peaceful. As we floated silently through Yurok land, Claypole was the first to notice the coastal influence in the trees, vegetation and, in turn, birdlife. Instead of stumpy willows, which we found far upriver, the banks were lined with tan oaks, California laurel, and Port Orford cedar. Instead of slashing a path, the river now widened and rolled on through, carrying us at five or six miles per hour. In most eddies, the Indians had set monofilament gillnets, even though very few salmon migrate upriver in the spring.

I took my turn at the oars and Claypole looked hard at the map.

"We'll be out of Indian Country soon," Claypole said. Nobody had any intention of setting foot on the shoreline; that would not only have been basic trespassing, but also a violation of trust with the Indians.

We had no confrontations, not even a hint of one. In fact, since our expedition, much of the divisiveness between Indians and out-of-towners has now been resolved to the point that the Hoopa Indian Reservation welcomes visitors to its museum, and also arranges historical tours and rafting trips on the Trinity River. On the reservation, you simply don't feel the tensions that once were so common. Violence has become rare. At the same time, the Indians have won a legal claim to a large share of the salmon on the Klamath, which has done much to diffuse the antagonism.

"Look!" shouted Claypole. He pointed at a tiny bird ahead of us. "It's a surf scooter. We can't be far now." The countdown was on—14 miles to go.

Even at the Highway 101 bridge, just a few miles from the Pacific, the river current was pushing us on. Dozens of harbor seals and sea lions were all around us, jumping and snorting like a greeting party. Yuroks netting candlefish along the shoreline stared at us, then went back to work. Others were catching lampreys.

The feared north winds of spring had gone to sleep. Instead of getting pushed back, we paddled on, sensing the end. You could smell the ocean salt and taste it in the air.

We oared around a bend, and there was the ocean! It was calm and clear, the sun just about to set, a perfect picture. The outgoing tide was swallowing us into the sea, the raft bobbing in the swells.

"Stay hard to the left," Claypole shouted to the oarsmen in the other rafts, "or the tide will get you!"

We could taste our victory. Claypole reached with the oars, caught a wave and surfed the raft onto the beach. I jumped out, up to my knees in saltwater with the bow line. The other two boats were right with us.

Claypole grabbed a bottle of champagne and laughed. "If I'd known I was gonna live this long, I would have taken better care of myself."

Around the campfire that night, the six of us tried to outdo each other as to who was the wettest, coldest, tiredest and hungriest. We'd passed a thousand rapids, covered 45 to 55 miles per day, been kicked out, swallowed and digested by the river.

"I could skin a bear and eat him raw," said Kurt Rogers. "Then I'd crawl headfirst into my sleeping bag and pass out."

But there came the realization that the longer we stayed on the river, the less important seemed the merit of any of the "firsts" on the trip. What developed instead was a feeling of oneness with our surroundings that bonded the six of us.

Every leaf seemed to speak a language. The sound of the river was the mountain song. It was the Klamath bringing the north country alive. Having felt it, seen it and lived it was the real victory.

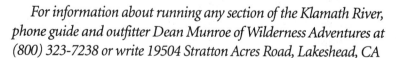

For information about running any section of the Klamath River, phone guide and outfitter Dean Munroe of Wilderness Adventures at (800) 323-7238 or write 19504 Stratton Acres Road, Lakeshead, CA 96051.

Up a snowfield on the way to Lake Helen on Mount Shasta

Climbing
MOUNT SHASTA

Peak Experience

❖

Shasta is a mountain of fire and ice, a place where you can find a challenge and an answer, both mysteries and truths. The challenge is the climb and the answer is that you can likely complete it. The mysteries are of Lemurians, Yaktayvians and Phylos, creatures who are said to inhabit the inner mountain. The truth is only for you to find.

At 14,162 feet, Mount Shasta rises like a giant diamond in a field of coal. Located 60 miles north of Redding, it is the jewel of Northern California, and can sometimes be seen for more than a hundred miles in all directions. U.S. Forest Service scientist Michael Furniss, photographer John Storey, my brother Rambob and I planned to reach the top of it in a single day.

Climbing Shasta is one of the West's great adventures, an endurance test that most people in good physical condition have an honest chance of achieving. Climbing Half Dome in Yosemite or hiking the Grand Canyon might be comparable outdoor achievements. But Shasta stands apart because of its sheer size—with a volume of 80 cubic miles, it's the highest of Northern California's peaks, the largest of the Cascade volcanoes. Much of it is gouged with glacial canyons.

To put it straight, the climb to Shasta's peak can be a punishing hike, an ascent of 7,000 feet over ice, snow and rock—while trying to suck what little oxygen you can out of the thin air. The big stopper is weather. The old mountain creates its own, and a sudden whiteout can turn your trip into a blackout, even in summer. Mountain sickness, a combination of dizziness, nausea and wheezing, also claims its share of victims. If you're trying to make the summit in one day, the clock can work against you—there is a maximum of 14 hours of daylight in summer, less at other times of the year.

According to the U.S. Forest Service, about half of those who try don't make it, with bad weather being the number one preventive factor. That's why we chose to make our trip in early August, when Shasta gets its mildest weather of the year.

John Muir made it to the top. So did Josiah Whitney, the country's leading geologist in the late 1800s. Thousands of others have since tried. Your success or failure in reaching the peak may depend on forces well beyond your own control. "Man is not always a welcome visitor in a kingdom he cannot control," said mountaineer Fred Beckey, describing Shasta.

At Mount Shasta, you are a visitor at one of the world's true cathedrals. As at any sacred place, you become aware that not all are permitted to enter.

We made our base camp at 7,400 feet. At daybreak, we looked up at the old mountain through branches of red fir. Red Bank, a jagged outcrop at 12,900 feet, seemed almost straight up, preceded by a 4,000-foot ice field. There are many routes to the peak, but most people start the trip at Horse Camp, a two-mile hike in from road's end at 6,800 feet on the southwestern side of the mountain. At Horse Camp you can get water, set up a base camp for the trip and prepare for the ascent.

From here, figure it will take eight or nine hours of scrambling to reach the peak and three or four hours to get back. Leaving at 5:30 a.m., you can be back by sunset—if all goes well, that is. Many depart far earlier. When Josiah Whitney climbed Shasta with William Brewer in 1862, they left at 2 a.m. after a moonlit breakfast.

At Horse Camp, well before first light, we hid our large backpacks in the forest. We strapped on small daypacks that carried food, emergency weather gear and snow equipment. The first few steps seemed so easy, a gentle climb over brown rocks, which looked like much of the pumice that covers Shasta from its last eruption 300 years ago. The small porous rocks formed from lava that blew right out of the top like puffed wheat.

"You can't get lost going up Shasta," said my brother Rambob. "Any direction going up is the right direction."

The last trees disappeared at 8,500 feet, and as we entered the alpine area, only a few tiny flowers were sprinkled among the rocks, wherever they could find a toehold. This late in summer, the first snow was at 8,600 feet. A little patch of it sat at the bottom of a gully, fingers of it tracing up the mountainside.

Already, the world below seemed to be opening up at our feet. Looking south, we could view the entire Sacramento River canyon, topped by Castle Crags, a series of granite spires near Dunsmuir. The sun wasn't up yet, but its glow lightened the tops of the Marble Mountains 40 miles to the west. Below in the valley, at 2,800 feet, we could make out cars and trucks traveling on Interstate 5, tiny images in the distance. I remembered how many times I had driven the highway, then looked up to Shasta, wondering if a day would come when I would climb it. That day had come.

At 9,100 feet, we reached the start of a long, narrow cut packed with ice and snow called Climber's Gully, and stopped to strap crampons on our boots. Crampons are metal frames with spikes, which dig into the ice to hold your position.

I jammed my ice ax in the slope, sensed its hold, then pulled myself up a step, booted crampons holding the gain. My short steps made a crunch-crunch sound as I began climbing the ice slope. The going was slow. A few steps, a few breaths, and I'd continue on. It was so quiet, I could almost hear my heart beat. The ice field seemed to stretch on forever, and my ice ax was holding each step. But I had an eerie feeling, as if I were being watched. Other people up here have had the same sensation.

"Look at that!" shouted Furniss, the scientist. Thousands and thousands of dark moths had hatched and were fluttering along the slope, so many that you could hear their wingbeats. It is the only time I have seen such a phenomenon.

Stranger things have been reported on Shasta. A species of mysterious beings known as Lemurians are said to inhabit the inner world of the mountain. According to legend, they live in underground caves that are lined with gold. Some people say the Lemurians are tiny, while others identify them as huge, perhaps seven or eight feet tall.

Phylos is the most famous Lemurian. He is said to be able to materialize at will, wearing a flowing white robe. A climbing party once claimed that they were invited into his golden temple to listen to soft music. But at 10,000 feet we still hadn't seen any sign of Phylos.

Then there are the Yaktayvians of the Secret Commonwealth. They are said to have built the greatest bells in the universe, tuned so precisely that their ring causes giant landslides. Some people claim to have heard the bells while driving on Highway 5. We're still listening.

Maybe it was the Yaktayvians who caused the rockslide we passed at Helen Lake. The lake is actually only a flat depression at 10,440 feet, occasionally the site for a shallow pond in late summer when ice melts above it. It's one of the few spots where climbers can set up a camp, although it can be cold. It was about 20 degrees here during our climb, on a day when it reached 105 in Redding. High winds are also common here. When we arrived, we were told that a rock the size of a Volkswagen had come tumbling down through the area the previous night.

After a lunch of jerky, nuts, dried fruit and water, we moved on. At 12,000 feet, the slope reaches 35 degrees and each step is a labor of passion. You jam your ice ax in the snow, pull yourself up a step, then rest for a moment before repeating the process. With long-spiked crampons, the steps come easier, the metal tips poking holes and grabbing the icy slope.

It is below Red Bank, a huge red volcanic outcrop, where Shasta chews up most of its climbers. Some people start to wonder why they're even here. Fun? Who said this was fun? It seems too steep. One slip and you might turn into a human snowball. Many turn around and return to Horse Camp.

A few more steps, a few more breaths. It was near here during Whitney's geologic expedition in 1862 that three members of the team got mountain sickness and were barely able to continue. On this trip, our scientist, Furniss, was having the same problem. His face was so bleached that he looked like he'd seen a Lemurian.

"Dizzy, very dizzy," Furniss said. He slowed his pace, but continued. At Red Bank, you must scramble through a steep rock and ice chute where you would certainly fall without crampons. We forged through, then emerged atop Red Bank, perched at 13,000 feet. Close, very close.

We crossed a lumpy glacier and forged ahead toward what is known as Misery Hill, because it gives the false impression of being the summit. When you rise atop the hill, however, the true Shasta peak suddenly rises before you, a massive pinnacle of lava which seems to jut straight up into the air.

The air is thin and your lungs gasp for all they can get, but it is never enough. At the top, the Shasta summit, there is no snow. Wind has carried it away. Your steps are slow, but now you can see the goal. With a final push, your hands grabbing rock to pull you up this pinnacle, you take the last few steps, and suddenly you are standing on top.

A lot of things can make you shout, but standing on top of a big mountain is something that can make you silent. Just over there is Shastina, Shasta's smaller volcano, a glaciated turquoise pond forming a bowl in its mouth. To the north are miles of Oregon, the Three Sisters Mountain Peaks barely visible through binoculars. On those rare perfectly clear days up here, you can see Mount Hood, Mount Lassen, the Siskiyou's backbone and 200 miles beyond.

On the day of our climb, clouds obscured the view. Some light hailstones fell, looking like little puffs of cotton. At 14,000 feet, the sky is a deeper blue than you've ever seen, and on this day, scarcely a hint of wind was blowing.

From the side of the peak, a plume of sulfurous smoke still rises from inside the old volcano. In 1875, John Muir almost froze to death when he was caught in a blizzard at Shasta's peak. He stayed alive by spending a night huddled near the mountain's hot sulfur gas vents.

As we were perched on top, I thought of Muir standing at the same point. And of Whitney's trip. And of the thousands of other hikers who have since climbed Northern California's greatest peak. You will sense their shadows, and sometimes maybe even their ghosts, helping you as you pull your way up the old mountain.

Questions about Shasta

Answers to the 10 most frequently asked questions about climbing Mount Shasta:

1—Is it necessary to have any mountaineering experience to climb Mount Shasta? No, in fact, only about 20 percent of those who try have mountain climbing experience. What is necessary is to be in good physical condition.

2—What special equipment is necessary? Be certain to bring a hat, sunglasses, sunscreen, ice ax, crampons for boots, and a day pack containing food, a map and foul weather gear. A wilderness permit from the U.S. Forest Service is required.

3—How long is the climb from Horse Camp? From Horse Camp to the summit is only about five miles, but with an elevation gain of 7,000 feet. People who successfully reach the peak do so in about eight hours.

4—How long does it take to return from the peak to Horse Camp? Usually about four hours, a bit more quickly if you ski or slide (which rangers do not advise).

5—To shorten the climb, can you camp higher on the mountain? Yes, you can camp at 10,440 feet at Helen Lake, which is actually a flat area, but this involves carrying all your camping gear up a long steep snowfield called Climber's Gully.

6—What are the most dangerous problems of the climb? Getting marooned at a high elevation during a sudden snow storm can lead to hypothermia. The most serious injuries are caused when rolling boulders strike climbers. Climbers without crampons and ice axes can slip and fall at the chute at Red Bank.

7—How many days should I plan for the trip? Most people who set up a base camp will spend two nights on the mountain, with one day for the ascent to the top and the return to the base camp.

8—How many people will I see? On weekends, an average of 15 to 20 people will attempt the climb, fewer on weekdays.

9—How much water should I carry? A minimum of two quarts, with plans to refuel at 13,000 feet in the chute at Red Bank. Water is the lifeblood of the trip, and we drank three to four quarts apiece.

10—Who do I contact to rent equipment, or for maps and more information? The Fifth Season in the town of Mount Shasta rents ice axes and crampons, and also sells an excellent guide map. They can be reached by phoning (916) 926-3606. A 24-hour climbing report is available by phoning (916) 926-5555. For area maps, guide services, lodging and information, call Shasta Cascade at (800) 326-6944. There is no fee for wilderness permits, which must be obtained in person from the Mount Shasta Ranger District at (916) 926-4511.

If you want to climb Shasta but don't want to go it alone, contact

Shasta Mountain Guides. Phone Michael Zanger at (916) 926-3117 or write to 1938 Hill Road, Mt. Shasta, CA 96067.

More Mountains to Climb

If you're looking for other peaks to challenge, here are two other California climbing favorites:

•**Mount Whitney, 14,496 feet**—This is the Big One, the highest point in America's lower 48. It's a long steep hike from the trailhead at Whitney Portal, climbing 6,100 feet in 10 miles. But a decent trail takes you to the top, so no mountaineering equipment is necessary, although crampons help greatly over snowfields.

Whitney is located in the southern Sierra above the town of Lone Pine on Highway 395. It's a giant rock cut by glaciers, not formed from a volcano like Shasta and Lassen, and the peak reflects it—sheer rock outcrops on the edge of dramatic, plunging canyons.

Nothing can prepare you for the lookout. It is absolutely astonishing. To the west is the entire Western Divide, to the north are rows of 11,000- to 13,000-foot peaks, and to the east the mountain drops straight down—an 11,000-foot drop in just 15 miles—to the Owens Valley. The top itself is oval with a jagged edge, with a little rock house constructed to protect hikers from storms.

The hike is a genuine heart-thumper, yet inspiring at the same time. It includes 100 switchbacks to climb Wotan's Throne, and in the final miles, the ridge is cut by notch windows in the rock. You look through and the bottom drops thousands of feet at your boot tips. Some people try the 20-mile round-trip in one day, but that makes it an exhausting rush, dangerous at such high altitudes. A better strategy is to hike in and set up a base camp at 10,000 feet, getting acclimated to the altitude. The next day, you can hit the top and return, carrying a minimum of equipment for the ascent. A wilderness permit from the U.S. Forest Service is required.

•*Notes:* Bring pain relievers for high altitude headaches, good hiking boots, warm weather gear in a daypack, along with plenty of water, high energy snacks, sunglasses, sunscreen and a hat. It is advisable to set up an overnight camp at Trail Camp, dividing the hike into two pieces. Contact Inyo National Forest Mount Whitney Ranger District in Lone Pine for a wilderness permit, maps and information; phone (619) 876-5542.

•**Mount Lassen, 10,457 feet**—This is a good introduction to mountain climbing. The summit climb is a two-and-a-half-mile zigzag of a hike that just about anybody with a quart of water can handle, yet provides one of the most spectacular peaks anywhere.

You can drive to the trailhead at the base of the mountain set in Lassen Volcanic National Park, 50 miles east of Red Bluff. The trail surface is hard and flat, so you can get into a nice hiking rhythm, and with a 15-percent grade, it isn't a killer. Most people take under two hours to reach the top, about a 2,000-foot elevation gain. In the process, though, newcomers often ask themselves, "Why am I doing this?" When they reach the crest, they find out.

The view is superb, with the awesome Mount Shasta 100 miles north appearing close enough to reach out and grab. To the east are hundreds of miles of forests and lakes, with Lake Almanor a surprise jewel, and to the west, the land drops off to several small volcanic cones and the Central Valley.

The peak itself is the top of a huge volcanic flume and you can spend hours probing craters and hardened lava flows. Lassen last blew its top in a series of eruptions from 1914 to 1921, which in geologic time is only a few minutes ago.

It's a prime first mountain experience. We met people of all ages and in all kinds of physical shape. If you bring water and get an early start, like by 8:30 a.m., you'll probably make it. It's that simple.

•*Notes:* Bring at least a quart of water, a windbreaker, sunglasses, sunscreen and a hat, and get an early start to beat the heat. Note that Lassen Park will probably establish a hiker quota for this trail in the not-too-distant future. Contact the park before planning to set out for the climb. For a map and information, phone Lassen National Park at (916) 595-4444.

Tom and Michael Furniss take in the beautiful waterfall that blocked their path as they trekked in to Little South Fork Lake.

Miles from
NOWHERE

Excursions into Remote California

❖

The rocky chute rose almost straight up, and from our perch on a narrow ledge, it seemed like we were trying to climb the backbone of a huge monster. Below was a 1,500-foot wall of rock, above was the Sawtooth Ridge of the Trinity Alps. We were climbing off-trail, in search of wonders, unknown lakes and big trout, ready for mystery and danger.

Rivers, lakes and oceans will attack you. Mountains are different. They wait for you to make a mistake.

I reached up and grabbed hold of a rock, and it gave way and went crashing down the talus slope like a bowling ball. My heart shook at the thought that our bodies could do the same.

Then I remembered my old wilderness adage: Don't fight the mountain. Accept it, think it through and move forward. Deep inside of you, right in your chest, is a window, and when the window opens, the power of the universe will flow through you. Don't let the window shut and lock. Settle down and let it open.

With that thought, feeling more settled, I grabbed another rock. It held. I pulled myself up, a booted foot lodged in a crevice for support. A light breeze coming up the canyon made the sweat tingle on the back of my neck. The next foot came easier. Made it through a tough spot, just like that.

We scrambled to the mountain rim and peered from a ridge

notch as if we were standing on the edge of the earth. Below us in all directions was the Trinity Alps Wilderness, northwest of Redding, immense wildlands with 585,000 acres, 82 lakes, 50 mountain peaks and 550 miles of trails. It is one of America's greatest wilderness lands.

The biggest mountain-bred rainbow trout of the West live here in remote, little-known lakes. But to reach them, you must leave the trail. One such lake, Little South Fork Lake, is said to have trout that average 15 to 18 inches, some of the largest high mountain trout anywhere. But in a guidebook for the area, author Wayne Moss called reaching this lake "a task for deranged souls."

That made me a perfect candidate, along with my pals and fellow wilderness explorers Jeff Patty and Michael Furniss. Patty and Furniss aren't quite over the edge, but they are a bit crazy. The idea of giant rainbow trout in remote wildlands was enough to inspire another trip, no matter how challenging.

The Trinity Alps may be the prettiest land in the western United States. The granite chutes on the mountain rims make them look like the Swiss Alps. The lakes are set in classic granite bowls. Every deep canyon looks like a sea of conifers.

From the trailhead at Coffee Creek, we hiked in 12 miles to the Caribou Lakes Basin, spent the night, then stared hard at the map, studying the terrain and slope.

"There's no easy way in to Little South Fork Lake," Patty said. "No easy way out."

"Perfect for three deranged souls," answered Furniss.

Our plan was to drop down to Little South Fork Creek, then follow it upstream to the lake. It seemed simple enough. Of course, it wasn't.

There would be an altitude drop of 2,500 feet, then a climb of 3,500 feet without the benefit of a trail. In our way were two mountains, and we decided to lateral around them, taking bear paths and deer trails to do it. It wasn't long until we ran into a massive brush field, and we three deranged souls disappeared into it, one after another. We grappled with branches, scrambled for toeholds, fell down and cursed the brush. After several hours, our forearms were scratched up like we'd been in a fight with a pack of bobcats and gotten the worst of it.

"Getting caught in that brush makes you feel like a bug in a spiderweb," Furniss said.

But there's no fighting it, I thought to myself. You lose every time. Remember the window in your chest. Let it open and you can move on.

Later, after dropping elevation and heading through a forest, Patty spotted what looked like a bear trail, and we were able to take one good step after another for the first time in hours. The air smelled of pines and we could faintly hear the sound of a small stream. I took a deep breath and felt like I was back in the 1830s when the first trailblazers came west.

Right then, there was a terrible stinging sensation on my right hand. Then—bang! Again, in my arm. And again, right in the butt. I looked down at my stinging arm and hand and saw bees swarming around me. I let out a howl, and in a flash, I unhitched my pack and went running through the forest, then stopped to see if I had outrun them. No such luck. Some 20 bees were clamped onto my pants, trying to sting my legs. Others were circling around my head.

"They've marked you, they've marked you," shouted Furniss. "Run, run!"

In a panic-stricken rush, I swept them off my legs, and went running through brush and around trees. I would have given a million dollars for a lake to jump in, but there was no lake. A minute later, after being chased by a swarm, I eluded them in a brush thicket, and it was over.

Patty, certified for emergency medical treatment, immediately grabbed me.

"Do you have allergic reactions to bee stings?"

"No," I answered, and then he slid the stingers out, using care not to break the poison sacks.

"You must have stepped on a hive," Furniss said. "You're lucky you didn't get stung a hundred times."

"A lot of people get hurt when they're running from a swarm of bees," Patty added. "In panic, they don't watch where they're going and break an ankle or a leg. Then, while laying there, the bees get them anyway."

Later, we dropped down the canyon stream, hoping to rock-hop straight up the river, eventually reaching the lake. The plan was working well until we ran head-on into a surprise, a 100-foot waterfall, unmarked on our map. We named it Crystal Falls, because the falling water droplets refracted by sunlight looked like crystals.

But as pretty as it was, that waterfall blocked our route. To get around it required backtracking, then scrambling up a 120-degree talus slope to gain altitude on the canyon wall, lateraling across thick brush, and climbing our way to the rim of a rock basin. It took us 10 hours to travel under two miles, but when we topped that rim we could finally see it, Little South Fork Lake.

It was just before sunset. Little South Fork Lake is a particularly beautiful lake— small, but deep blue and surrounded by steep, glaciated granite walls. Even from a distance, we could see the insects hatching and the trout rising.

After a night of recovery, we made our first casts. In my first seven casts, I had five strikes and landed rainbow trout measuring 12, 13 and 16 inches. The biggest catch of the trip was 17.5 inches. I had another one that ripped off 20 feet of line in two seconds before spitting the hook. That's never happened to me anywhere else in high mountain wilderness.

Yes, the fish were as big as we'd been told. And there is a logical explanation for it. Even though the Trinity Alps look like the top of the world, the elevations are 5,000 to 6,000 feet, much lower than the Sierra Nevadas or the Rocky Mountains.

"That's why there is more terrestrial productivity here than in the high Sierra," said Furniss, who is a soil and water scientist.

"There is more soil, more trees, more algae in the bottom of lakes and more insect hatches."

In other words, there is more life in general, including fish. Big ones. There was no "evening rise," like at most lakes. The fish were feeding continuously.

At night, there was a remarkable calm at this remote lake. Deer, sometimes 15 at a time, could be seen ambling by in the bright moonlight, within 10 yards of the camp.

Patty pointed to the granite rim above the lake. "When it's time to get out of here, let's climb that," he said. "No way do we want to fight the brush, the bees and that waterfall again."

Patty smiled and started suggesting possible routes. Nearby, a big trout jumped and landed with a splash. Fifty yards away, a deer started at the surprise visitors, the three deranged souls.

Furniss sized up the ridge, bright in the moonlight, and smiled.

"It looks just about impossible to climb," he said with a laugh.

A minute later, he spoke again.

"Perfect."

Marble isn't usually thought of as a precious stone. But it is gem-like to any hiker who ventures into the Marble Mountain Wilderness in Northern California.

The area covers 230,000 acres of some of the West's greatest wildlands: 79 lakes, a thousand miles of remote trails that twist from deep forests to craggy ridgelines, and a series of great lookouts from hikes that follow mountain rims.

At the center of the wilderness is a mountain that nature has carved out of pure marble. Even from a distance, it has a different look to it than any mountain you've ever seen, jutting above treeline in a stark red/gray stone, sometimes speckled with fool's gold. The Pacific Crest Trail runs adjacent to Marble Mountain, allowing a smooth off-trail traipse to Marble Rim and its extraordinary views.

Yet Patty, Furniss and I did not enter without concern. You know the kinds of things people tell you: Will there be rain? *"Like monsoons."* Mosquitoes? *"They come in clouds."* Bears? *"A visit every night."* How are the trout? *"Spooky."* Camping seclusion? *"Expect plenty of company."* The trails? *"Mighty steep."*

Well, our experience turned out significantly different. We had no rain for a week, only three mosquito bites among us, didn't even see a bear, had trout for dinner every night, and encountered other campers on only three of seven days. In fact, we saw many more deer than people and camped in virtual seclusion at different lakes every night. And while the trails are steep enough to get you puffing for a while, they crest out soon enough, quite a respite from the endless grades in the Sierra Nevada that often rise 4,000 to 6,000 feet before reaching a pass.

The lakes are gems, each a rock bowl carved by nature long ago, then filled with snowmelt. They are also filled with brook, rainbow and brown trout. Our first camp was a late one, at Onemile Lake, and we didn't have much daylight left to catch a few fish for dinner. But my empty stomach said it was worth a try anyway, so I put on my favorite lure, a gold Met-L Fly. In 10 casts, I caught six trout, then quit. They were big enough that I had to cut the heads and tails off to fit them in the frying pan.

Another evening, at Spirit Lake, Jeff Patty announced he wanted two trout for dinner. So he made two casts with a yellow Roostertail and caught himself two trout. Michael Furniss once said that when it came to fishing, he was jinxed. Well, ol' Furniss caught and released so many trout that the only thing jinxed were the trout ending up in his stomach.

In fact, instead of catching trout and then throwing them back, there were times we'd just catch bugs and throw them on the water, and then we'd sit on a rock and bet over whose bug would last the longest before being eaten by a trout. Five minutes was the longest we had to wait.

We entered the Marble Mountain Wilderness from the southwest side, driving out on a logging road that starts near where the Salmon River enters the Klamath. After about a half hour of travel, we parked at the trailhead and started hiking. We covered about 50 miles in a week, hitting lakes such as Onemile, Ukonom, Spirit, Cuddihy and Pleasant, and spotting a half dozen others.

There are many options. The eastern portion of the wilderness, for instance, has more lakes and higher mountains. The northern trailheads have better access to Marble Mountain. Get a map and start looking—the possibilities are endless.

We added some spice to the trip by leaving the trail for a day of bushwhacking, primarily following animal trails and mountain rims. We left our backpacks behind on another day, hoofing it with a light daypack up to Marble Mountain to get a real taste of what this area is about.

On the trip back, we looped down Wooley Creek, a lush forested watershed, then turned off and headed for the trailhead. Suddenly, we saw a blue grouse hen in the trail, puffed up in defense, its wings sheltering a dozen chicks. We scrambled up a slope and around the little family. Some things, such as the grouse and its home in the Marble Mountain Wilderness, are best left undisturbed—to be discovered another day.

Opposite: Michael Furniss finds a rocky perch on the way to Marble Mountain.

I could not have been more lost. There I was, a guy who is supposed to know about these things, transfixed by confusion, snow and hoof prints from a big deer. I discovered it is actually quite easy to get lost. If you don't get your bearings, getting found is the difficult part.

This was in the Siskiyou Wilderness of northwestern California, where I'd hiked in to a remote lake called Devil's Punchbowl, and then set up a base camp for a deer hunt. I'd heard there were giant bucks in the area—but it would take a mountaineer to get even close to them.

That was a challenge I was prepared to take. After four-wheeling it to the trailhead, I tromped off with my pack and rifle, gut-thumped it up 100 switchbacks, climbed 2,000 feet over the rim, then followed a creek drainage up to a small but beautiful lake. The area near the Punchbowl is stark and almost treeless, with bald granite broken only by large boulders. To mark the path for the return trip, the route was dotted with piles of small rocks.

But at daybreak the next day, I stuck my head out of my tent and found eight inches of snow on the ground. I looked up into a gray sky filled by huge, cascading snowflakes. Visibility was about 50 yards, with fog on the mountain rim. "I better get out of here and get back to my truck," I said to myself. "If my truck gets buried at the trailhead, I'll never get out."

After packing quickly, I started down the mountain. But after 20 minutes, I felt disoriented. You see, all the little piles of rocks stacked to mark the way were now buried in snow. There was only a smooth white blanket to guide me. Low fog obscured all landmarks. Everything looked the same, and it was snowing even harder now.

Five minutes later I started chewing on some jerky to keep warm, then suddenly stopped. Where was I? Where was the creek drainage? Isn't this where I was supposed to cross over a creek and start the switchbacks down the mountain?

Right then I looked down and saw the tracks of a huge deer, the kind I'd heard about. What a predicament: Lost, snowed in, with big hoof prints in the snow. Part of me wanted to abandon all safety and go after that deer, but a little voice in the back of my head won out: "Treat this as an emergency," it said.

The first step in any predicament is to secure your present situation, to make sure it does not get any worse. I unloaded my rifle (too easy to slip, fall and have a misfire), took stock of my food (three days worth), camp fuel (plenty), and clothes (rain gear keeping me dry). Then I wondered, "Where the hell am I?"

I took out my map, compass and altimeter, opened the map and laid it on the snow. It immediately began collecting snowflakes. I set the compass on the map and oriented it to north. Because of the fog, there was no way to spot landmarks, such as prominent mountain tops, which could verify my position. Then I checked the altimeter: It read 4,900 feet. Well, the elevation at Devil's Punchbowl was 5,320 feet. That was critical information.

I scanned the elevation lines on the map and was able to trace the approximate area of my position, somewhere downstream from the lake, yet close to 4,900 feet elevation. "Right here," I said, pointing to a spot on the map. "I should pick up the switchback trail down the mountain somewhere off to the left, maybe just 40 or 50 yards away."

Slowly and deliberately, I pushed through the light, powdery snow. After five minutes, I saw it. To the left, across a 10-foot depression in the snow, was a flat spot that veered off to the right. "That's it! That's the crossing."

In minutes, I was working down the switchbacks, on my way, no longer lost. I thought of the hoof prints I had seen, and now that I knew my position, I wanted to head back and spend the day hunting. Then I looked up at the sky, saw it filled with falling snowflakes, and envisioned my truck buried deep in snow. Alas, logic won out over dreams.

In a few hours, now trudging through well more than a foot of snow, I was at my truck at a spot called Doe Flat, and next to it was a giant all-terrain U.S. Forest Service vehicle and two rangers.

"Need any help?" I asked them.

They just laughed. "We're here to help *you*," one answered. "It's a good thing you filed a trip plan with our district office in Gasquet. We wouldn't have known you were out here."

"Winter has arrived," said the other. "If we don't get your truck out now, it will be stuck here until next spring. If we hadn't found you, you might have been here until the end of time."

They connected a chain from the rear axle of their giant rig to the front axle of my truck and started towing me out, back to civilization. On the way to pavement, I figured I had gotten the lessons of my life: Always file a trip plan. Have plenty of food, fuel and a camp stove you can rely on. Make sure your clothes, weather gear, sleeping bag and tent will keep you dry and warm. Always carry a compass, altimeter and map with elevation lines, and know how to use them, practicing in good weather to get the feel of it.

And if you get lost and see the hoof prints of a giant deer, well, this is one time it's probably best to pass them by. Seeing Devil's Punchbowl in a blizzard will never let you forget it.

A white pelican glided overhead as I made my first cast of the morning, the big bird scanning for a stray fish for breakfast. It was daybreak at Lake Almanor, with first light brightening the eastern horizon.

The pelican landed on a boulder, and both the bird and I watched the fishing line settle on the quiet lake surface like a string of little curlicues, then begin to sink. Suddenly, the line straightened and the rod tip twitched.

I pointed the rod at the water, trying to put a little slack in the line, but again the line was tugged. You could feel it. Nibble-nibble, nibble-nibble. Something was there and I set the hook hard—and felt the power of a big fish on the other end. The pelican went airborne for a closer look.

The fish was no minnow. It streaked 50 yards, jumped, burrowed down to the bottom of the lake, crossed under the boat, came up on the other side and jumped again, then ran off another 40 yards of line. After 10 minutes, I led it to the side of the boat. The pelican took one look and returned to his rock: Way too big for his breakfast.

It was a king salmon, a seven-pounder, the kind that coastal fishermen search the ocean for. But this was Lake Almanor, not the Pacific Ocean. That combination—king salmon in a lake—has made Lake Almanor one of the biggest fishing spots in the West.

Lake Almanor is located in the mountain country of northern Plumas County, just southeast of Lassen National Park. Many vacationers have missed it because it is set between Shasta Lake and Lake Tahoe, the two top vacation destinations in Northern California. Plumas County has far more deer than people in an area of 2,500 square miles. Yet there are more than 60 campgrounds, 100 lakes and 1,000 miles of streams. The Gold Lakes Basin in Plumas National Forest is similar in geological makeup to the Desolation Wilderness west of Tahoe, with granite basin terrain and dozens of lakes in glacial rock bowls, but the area gets about one-tenth of Tahoe's use.

Almanor is the centerpiece to the area, a big beautiful lake, 13 miles long and six miles wide, nearly always full to the brim and circled by a conifer forest. It is fed not only by the Feather River, but also by the underground waterways of Mount Lassen, cold springs that bubble from lava tubes into the lake year around.

The salmon were first stocked in the 1980s by the Department of Fish and Game, which obtained the brood stock from Lake Michigan. Since then an average of 70,000 fish have been stocked per year. They join a resident population of large trout. All it takes is to hook one of them and you suddenly understand the fascination.

The salmon and trout can be difficult to find. Often you catch

Michael Furniss surveys the view in the Marble Mountain Wilderness.

just one or two a day, but they are almost always big, really big. If you get lucky and connect in a spree, you'll be tossing coins in the lake and praising Jonah.

"In 40 years of freshwater fishing, I've never experienced anything like it," said Bill Brantley, on vacation from Southern California. Brantley caught a limit of five fish that weighed a total of forty-and-a-half pounds—all salmon and brown trout weighing seven to nine pounds.

In a five-day span, our fishing guide Dan Barkhimer caught 97 salmon, often reaching the limit (five per angler) before the sun cleared the treetops. His biggest weighed 12 pounds, two ounces.

"You get one of those 10-pounders on and they'll take you all over the lake," Barkhimer said. "They'll run 70, 80 yards at a time. If they get around an anchor rope, they'll break off so fast and be gone that it'll kill you."

Key to the health of the fishery are the underwater springs and the hordes of pond smelt in the lake. The underwater springs keep the lake filled with water that is crystal clear, pure, oxygenated and cold. The pond smelt provide a vast food source for the salmon, similar to what anchovies provide for salmon in the ocean.

The lake is so clear that anglers can see the flash from the sides of a salmon 15 to 20 feet deep. But that clear water can also cause problems for newcomers. Because the water is so clear, high-strength lines can be seen by the salmon and spook them off the bite. As a result, anglers familiar with Lake Almanor use line rated no heavier than four-pound test. Newcomers unfamiliar with this trick can go days without a bite.

The rigging is straightforward: Simply tie a No. 4 hook on the end of the line, then clamp on a large split shot for weight about 20 inches above the hook. For bait, use the tail section of an anchovy or a nightcrawler threaded on the hook and line. The bait is cast out, then allowed to sit just a few feet off the lake bottom. Another popular method is to use a crappie jig, sometimes called a Maribou

Jig, or a bass jig called a Gitzit. Anglers should let the jig sink to the bottom, then give it a jerk every few seconds.

We were on the lake at 5 a.m., made the 10-minute cruise to Big Springs, located just north of the Hamilton Branch, and then tried all three methods—anchovy tail, nightcrawler and Gitzit jig, and caught salmon on all three. In the morning, we hooked 13 salmon and landed four. Several were lost during fights that could make a strong man cry.

And by the way, that poor pelican watching us never did see a fish small enough for it to eat.

Some places will never change until the end of time. People are drawn to them because they provide a sense of permanence that can't be found anywhere else. I call it the "power of place."

In the remote Sierra Nevada, there are such places, ageless and eternal, with the kind of natural beauty that makes you feel like the entire region has been molded by divine forces. This is the way it is at the headwaters of Rush Creek, where drops of melting snow gather near the Sierra crest at 10,500 feet, then run downhill for miles, through granite chutes, then into forest, rolling like a swirling emerald-green fountain.

Mountains shrines such as this are only accessible to visitors in mid-season. Spring arrives to the high Sierra in July, the snow finally melting away, allowing hikers to explore, camp and fish among the most pristine areas left in America.

Many of these mountain havens can be difficult to reach, and so it is at Rush Creek. A short visit requires a long drive to the trailhead in the June Lake Loop in the eastern Sierra, and then a demanding hike with a backpack, in the process contending with a 10-mile climb-out, ice-cold stream crossings, and frequent afternoon thunderstorms where lightning bolts and thunderclaps rattle off the canyon rims.

But as difficult as it seems to reach the high country, it is a physical challenge that can be met. For many, it becomes more difficult to leave. Why would anyone want to leave a place that runs in perfect harmony?

Rush Creek is such a place. It starts well above treeline as a mere trickle, then in a matter of miles, it starts to build size and force heading east down the Sierra slope. By the time it enters a pine forest at 9,500 feet elevation, the stream is about 25 feet wide, bordered by lush grasses and lilies, rolling past with a gentle surge.

The closest trailhead is at Silver Lake, a 7,200-foot elevation, located in the June Lake Loop. After departing Silver Lake on foot, hikers follow the trail adjacent to Lower Rush Creek upstream toward the Ansel Adams Wilderness. After three miles, you arrive at beautiful Gem Lake at 8,052 feet. Seven miles beyond it is Waugh Lake at 9,424 feet.

Many visitors never get farther than that, opting to camp, swim and fish at Gem or Waugh lakes. But it is upstream of Waugh Lake where you can discover the headwaters of Rush Creek, along with the flawless beauty of the untouched high country.

I'll never forget the first evening we spent on this river. An hour before dusk, a sudden thunderstorm enveloped the canyon. Furniss, Patty and I tried to hide next to trees as lightning bolts rattled off the nearby canyon rim. Thunderclaps echoed down the canyon, louder than a crate of exploding dynamite. You could smell the burning ozone in the air. The rain pounded like a monsoon. Then, half an hour later, it was over, just like that, and when darkness took over, there were hundreds upon hundreds of stars gleaming above. I wish I could have saved that moment forever.

The next day, I scouted up and down the beautiful river. Downstream, golden trout, the prettiest trout in the world, were leaving little swirls on the surface, rising to feed. Every summer night, they do the same, just as when Muir first visited here. Upstream, above treeline, the drops of melting snow were sliding off rocks and forming little dribbles, gravity taking them downhill, feeding the stream. The tundra was mushy, with shaded areas still loaded with snow.

Some trails are sloppy, especially in the tundra above treeline, and the creek crossings are wet, with some of the little streams running too high to cross just by hopping from rock to rock. At the least, wear your boots sockless when crossing streams. Never go barefoot—the cold water will numb your feet, making a fall likely.

A better strategy is to try a little invention of mine. Cut two strips of skin-diving material (Neoprene) and glue Velcro to the ends of each piece. Then when it is time for a stream crossing, wrap each boot top. You can walk right across the stream without getting any water down your boot.

Another factor is the inevitable encounter with bears. With such a long winter, they are always hungry and active; they'd like nothing better than to get at your food stash. The first order of setting up camp is to find a sturdy limb on a tall tree for a counter-balanced bear-proof food hang. That done, the bears will give your camp a sniff and then move on without much of a thought.

But contending with bears, stream crossings, and short but intense afternoon thunderstorms are just part of Nature's challenge. When some campers talk of their difficulties, you don't know whether they are complaining or bragging. In any case, only rarely do their problems turn out to be the focal point of their adventure. What stays with you instead are the feelings you get when you visit a wilderness, places out of reach of most of people. Those feelings all start when one senses the "power of place."

The high Sierra has it. For me, sometimes there is nothing better than sitting on a boulder along Rush Creek, watching that pure water run past. It will stay this way forever, and I will always return.

For more information about the Rush Creek area, send $3 for a map of Inyo National Forest to Office of Information, U.S. Forest Service, 630 Sansome Street, San Francisco, CA 94111. Also ask for a free wilderness brochure.

For a map of the Trinity Alps Wilderness, send $3 to U.S. Forest Service, 630 Sansome Street, San Francisco, CA 94111. For information about trail conditions and wilderness permits, phone Shasta-Trinity National Forest Headquarters at (916) 246-5222.

To obtain a map of the Marble Mountain Wilderness, send $3 to Maps, U.S. Forest Service, 630 Sansome Street, San Francisco, CA 94111.

To obtain a map of Six Rivers National Forest and the Siskiyous, send $3 to Maps, U.S. Forest Service, 630 Sansome Street, San Francisco, CA 94111.

For information, maps and brochures on Lake Almanor and Plumas County, call (800) 326-2247 or write Box 11018, Quincy, CA 95971.

The crew of 14 sets out on a 400-mile river journey from Redding to San Francisco Bay. The boat, designed and built by Neil Rucker of Redding, was a 36-foot-8-inch, 850-pound replica of the canoe used by the Voyageurs, a band of trappers with the Hudson Bay Company of 200 years ago.

We
VOYAGEURS

Canoeing 400 Miles on the Sacramento River

❖

Saltwater splashed over the giant canoe and slapped our faces, as if Mother Nature was about to teach a final lesson to 14 souls who dared to challenge her.

After seven days and 400 miles of paddling down the majestic Sacramento River from Redding to San Francisco Bay—through 100-degree temperatures and 18-hour days, around hidden boulders and reinforcement bars poking up from concrete slabs, and against headwinds and tides—it was down to just the last two miles.

But as many predicted, it didn't look as if we were going to make it.

The strength had been squeezed from us as if we were a bunch of wrung-out rags. And the Bay was like a lion raging up and clawing at us, a 20-knot wind thrown in our faces, a strong incoming tide against us, and nothing on our side but the hope to finish what we had started.

San Francisco Bay was angry. Whitecaps slapped against and over the sides of the canoe, soaking us. The wind whipped the hats off our heads. We dug our paddles into the water as if we were digging graves. But there seemed to be no progress toward the promised land, Fisherman's Wharf, our destination after a week of hoeing water.

Just east of Alcatraz, we stroked for 10 furious minutes trying to reach the "Rock" for a rest stop. But with the tide pushing us back, instead we lost about 10 yards and were forced to change our course.

At the bow, weary Terry Rucker now put the wood in the water with newfound ferocity, reaching back into the depths of himself to find the strength, saltwater dripping from his sunglasses. He had paddled for 400 miles while hardly missing a stroke. "This is the kind of experience that makes you know you are alive," he said.

Succeeding at this wasn't going to be easy, but few things worth remembering are.

It was Neil Rucker of Redding, a history teacher, who envisioned building an extraordinary craft—a 36-foot-8-inch, 850-pound replica of the canoe used by the Voyageurs, a band of trappers with the Hudson Bay Company that explored the Canadian wilderness 200 years ago. You may have read the story of the Voyageurs in a history book. Rucker wanted to live it.

Building this canoe—the *West Wind*—started as a weekend project, but it escalated when the word circulated around Redding of Rucker's ultimate plan: a 400-mile trip to Fisherman's Wharf, all in just a week. The improbability, hardship and potential danger of such a voyage drew many people to help build his craft and allowed Rucker to make a careful selection of the crew who would attempt the trip.

"It will take a different quality of person to make this trip," Rucker said. The question is: Can people accustomed to modern conveniences match the endurance of the Canadian Voyageurs of 200 years ago? "It will be difficult, painful and a real challenge. But if we make it, we'll get something special out of it, something that can only be known by doing it."

From the outset, the crew seemed bonded by an intense wish to strip off the coatings that smother much of American life and to live on the barest essentials—and also to prove that there remains a breed with the strength and grit to take on an adventure seen by many as folly. The doubters were everywhere. After one day in the canoe, Ken Castle, an outdoors writer, couldn't quite conjure the vision of a successful voyage.

"I hope you make it," he said, before departing for a different assignment. "But just think about it: You're going to try and take a canoe through Carquinez Strait and across San Francisco Bay? It can be hell out there with those tides and winds. But like I said, good luck." He smiled at me as if I were suffering from some rare form of mental aberration. Turns out I was—I was possessed by what I knew was to come in each day's adventure.

Others shook their heads and said something about our being "crazy." They were right.

"Remember that the Voyageurs were a mighty tough breed," said John Reginato, an old-timer outdoorsman who was born in 1918 at the river's headwaters in the small town of Delta, north of Redding. "To them, it was a matter of survival. Can modern man stand up to that? I'm not so sure. Others have tried and failed."

The Sacramento River starts as just a trickle at the base of Mount Shasta and rolls its way 400 river miles until it pours through the San Francisco Bay-Delta system and out the Golden Gate. It is joined by the Feather, Yuba, American and San Joaquin rivers and a number of tributaries, making it the mightiest waterway in California.

It's a thriving, gurgling and free-flowing river that offers bound-less recreational opportunities and miles of key habitat for fish, wildlife and birds. It's the source of water for the millions of water-fowl that come down the Pacific Flyway, as well as thousands of deer and salmon.

Tucked away inside every soul is the yearning for adventure. Like food and water, it's something you must have. For some, it takes a trip like this one to satiate that appetite. The lures of woods and water await. A 400-mile river adventure beckons.

Iron Canyon Rapids, south of Redding, is an unpredictable stretch of whitewater that has been known to eat canoes. It is set at the bottom of granite canyon walls, always waiting to hungrily swallow and digest unwary paddlers. For us and for the boat, it was our first major test.

How well the *West Wind* could handle Iron Canyon was unknown. After all, this was her maiden voyage, a freshly painted and untested craft, and nobody was placing any bets.

In Redding, we popped a champagne cork and toasted the Sacramento River, and then our captain, Neil Rucker, stood at the stern and barked out his first command. "Put the wood in the water," Rucker shouted and we were off, the craft sliding downstream through the water as if it were greased.

This was Day 1 on the voyage, and like the steady swing of a pendulum, our paddles dipped into the water in synchronization, steadily, but with power. The boat seemed to be propelled forward with an unexpected elegance, and members of the crew smiled at the sound of paddles dipping into the river and the fresh smell of morning. After just 15 minutes, we were already acquiring a feel for the pure and simple grace of the Sacramento River.

"Today we'll try for 70 miles," Rucker announced. "That means we'll take on Iron Canyon Rapids. That can get squirrelly, so be forewarned." He seemed tense, as if he envisioned his canoe wrapped around a boulder and snapped in two.

As Rucker spoke, a DC-9 jetliner was passing overhead. From the window of that jet, the Sacramento River must have looked quite a bit different than it did to the eyes of the 14 Voyageurs in the *West Wind*.

From that compartment some 30,000 feet above, you'd miss out on the great blue heron hovering just 40 feet from us, the beaver thundering the river surface with a slap of its tail, then suddenly disappearing, and the giant splash and swirl from a leaping 25-pound salmon. And as that DC-9 jet zipped out of view at 300 miles per hour, it was a symbol of the price we pay in trade for speed and progress. It is easy to miss out on a lot. But at least for a week, 14 Voyageurs hoped to reach back and rediscover the ruggedness of life, the grit that was taken for granted when the explorers first blazed west some 200 years ago. Watching over us were Mount Shasta to the north and Mount Lassen to the east, each feeding the river with its snowmelt, and each a testimonial that it is nature, not man, which can endure best through time.

How well our canoe would endure was another matter. A canoe's handling capabilities can be drastically affected by how burdened it is with weight—you can't load a canoe as if it is the *Queen Mary.* And especially not if you're heading for Iron Canyon Rapids.

After equipment duplications were discarded, the *West Wind* was loaded with about 3,000 pounds of people and gear. Yet when we crossed a wide, shallow sandbar, we found it floated in just six inches of water. That amazing feat bolstered the crew's confidence in the boat as well as that of our leader, Rucker, who personally designed the craft.

After 50 miles of river, an abrupt silence replaced the initial enthusiasm among the crew. It was 105 degrees and we'd paddled all day. People were tired, their strokes were lacking bite, but no one dared to utter a negative word. It was apparent that crew members were starting to think, perhaps wondering if they had what it takes to paddle another 350 miles in 100-degree temperatures.

It was obvious from the first stroke, however, that one man who had what it takes was Tom Ward, a wiry Vietnam vet. As soon as the paddles hit the water for our first stroke in Redding, Ward led the surge at the bow, hitting the river with a consistency and power that never diminished. Never. His friends call him the Eighth Natural Wonder of the World. Later, we would find out why.

Downstream of Redding, the Sacramento River is not known for its whitewater rapids. There is just one—Iron Canyon Rapids, also known as China Rapids.

Iron Canyon was a spectacle, the prettiest sight in our first day of paddling, where the river has cut a jagged line through the steep red canyon walls. Hidden rocks and boulders cause the current to surge up in a series of three whirlpools—and the unwary canoeist can get spun around, then dunked in a flash. With word of our arrival, county sheriffs had sent a rescue/patrol boat to the rapids. It was positioned in the calm water below the last big boulder, as if waiting to pick up any stray pieces that might come floating by. We entered the head of the rapids on alert.

"All back," shouted our captain, instructing us to slow down the craft, and we responded in unison, back paddling.

But it was the river who was boss. The current whipped us through the canyon, the bubbling freshwater splashing off our arms. We rocked like a teeter-totter through the froth. Astute paddle work by Ward at the bow and Rucker at the stern—guiding this overgrown canoe like a hook-and-ladder fire truck—kept us from being turned around by the whirlpools and crashing into one of the boulders.

We shot out of the chute like a bottle rocket and into calm water. We'd made it. The sheriff in the patrol boat almost seemed disappointed, but the giant canoe handled the big water perfectly, as if it was 1780 and was being paddled by the real Voyageurs. Only 350 miles to go.

After paddling a mere 50 miles, my shoulder felt like an alligator was gnawing at it, like there was a piece of gravel rolling around in the socket. The vultures circling overhead didn't make it feel any better.

"Keep stroking, but do it lightly, and it'll work out," advised Neil Rucker. There was no way anybody could stop, not with the endless river ahead. Our paddles raised and stroked in perfect unison, almost like those of Norsemen. Alas, it was so hot that Captain Rucker drank a candy bar. We pulled over along the bank, where a man was sitting in the shade of a cottonwood tree.

"How hot is it?" I asked.

"One hundred twenty at the homestead," he answered. "Hottest day of the year. I was hoping it'd be cooler down here by the river."

After 70 miles, our strokes hit the river with a new consistency and the pain in my shoulder had disappeared. But the sun was already branding us various shades of red. On the shoreline to our left, a band of buzzards eyed the strange craft.

"Those guys ought to be waiting for us at Alcatraz," said Voyageur Neil Babcock. But Captain Rucker didn't laugh. "There are enough snags in the water right here to make it tough on us in a hurry," he said.

"What do you mean?" I asked.

He just pointed along the river bank, and instantly I saw.

There are vicious, sharp steel rods embedded in concrete blocks that wait in ambush for canoes along the upper reaches of the Sacramento River. They can spike your boat, go right through your seat and impale you like a human shish kebab. Meanwhile, your canoe sinks. Very quickly. And these booby traps seemed to have signs on them saying "Welcome Voyageurs." A trip could be wiped out in just the moment it takes to ram into some terrible submerged object. That thought alone should have been enough to keep one alert, right? Not so.

The magical surroundings of the 100 miles of river below Red Bluff can easily put you in a state of mind where all danger is forgotten.

It's a wildlife paradise. An osprey hovers overhead, probing the sparkling river below for its next meal. Like a lightning bolt, the bird crashes to the river. They never seem to miss. The bird flies away slowly, with a trout in its talons.

On the nearby bank, a few deer take a break and sip at water's edge—while in the background a cottontail rabbit flashes up at our presence, then disappears into the brush. I even saw a family of a half dozen wild turkeys, hopping in a bluff above the river. Then there were the five turkey vultures sitting on a dead tree, having a staff meeting, perhaps deciding where they should wait for us.

This magnificent stretch of river is from Red Bluff to Colusa, where you can leave society behind and immerse yourself in the nature all around you, whether it is a trout rolling in the stream or the lush canopy of the riverside trees. It is a delicate place where a single person in a vast world can still seem significant.

The native vegetation at the river banks provides a habitat for numerous wildlife. Deer, beavers, river otters, possum, raccoons, skunks, squirrels, pheasant, valley tail, mourning doves, herons, turkey vultures, woodpeckers, jays, ducks, kingfishers, ospreys and eagles…the list is endless. For animals, there is opportunity to find a habitat of peace, sheltered in streamside tangles of large sycamore, black walnut, cottonwood and willow trees, as well as wild grape-vines, blackberry brambles and various grasses and weeds.

A silence crept over the crew in appreciation of what was unfolding around us. There are many exciting things which can cause wild cheer, but how many can inspire silent awe? Nature is one that can.

And as we rolled down the river, an old song rang through my head, over and over again, my paddle strokes keeping time.

Cool river breeze, like peppermint trees
that takes me back.
Chewing on a straw, torn overalls

cane pole and old straw hat.
Old river—just like a long, lost friend.
Roll on old river,
you make me feel like a child again.

This dream world suddenly vanished. There was a terrible gnawing sound as something scraped the bottom of our canoe, snapping the 14 Voyageurs back to reality. If it was a rebar, we could be sunk in an instant, the canoe destroyed.

A what?

A rebar, which is short for "reinforcement bar," a big chunk of concrete with several steel rods poking out. Rebars were once used in the construction of bridges, and with several old spans washed out along the river, they lie waiting underwater for the unsuspecting canoeist. They often can be spotted by an alert bow paddler, staring ahead of the boat for a swirl on the river surface that hints at what lies hidden below. Eagle-eye alertness is a necessity to assure detection. But this time, there was no signal.

As that scraping sound passed from bow to stern, I waited for the craft to be jolted, poked and snapped in two. My mind flashed back to a trip when, without warning, I hit a submerged concrete block in San Francisco Bay in an aluminum boat—and was thrown into the drink like a missile through the air. That boat sank.

That terrible scraping sound cut 37 feet down the length of the canoe. I could feel it under my feet. I held my breath. But then the scraping stopped. The only sound was that of rushing water.

No damage was done. "We were lucky this time," I said to Captain Rucker. He just nodded, still silent, still shaken.

The full moon hung like a specter over the Sacramento River, its dim light alone breaking the midnight darkness by which we wearily tried to find our way.

Three of the 14 Voyageurs were sprawled unconscious, exhausted from 17 straight hours of paddling through 100-degree temperatures on the river. The 11 others pushed on in eerie silence. But there was no place to stop.

Finally at 1:15 a.m., somewhere upstream of Knights Landing, our prayers were answered with a sandbar. We paddled over to the river bank, climbed out and collapsed on the beach. It was still so warm that nobody even bothered to unroll their sleeping bag. I had barely shut my eyes when Captain Bligh, er Rucker, was shaking my foot. "Time to get back on the river," he announced. "This was how the Voyageurs did it." It was 4:30 a.m., and we had only slept for three hours.

In a half hour, the canoe was loaded and we renewed our silent vigil with the river. We didn't stop until we reached Sacramento at 7 p.m. In a 36-hour stretch, we had paddled for 32 hours. What could cause such madness? Well, if you have ever seen the Sacramento River from Colusa to Sacramento, you would already know why 14 people apparently lost a grip on their mental facilities. We had to escape that horrendous place.

Approximately 150 miles of river has been stripped and raped by the Army Corps of Engineers, paid for by millions of tax dollars. It's an utter disgrace that our government has personally engineered the destruction of what was once a living paradise. Tons of rocks, concrete blocks and even car bodies have been dumped along the river's edge, destroying the riparian habitat and ensuring that the waterway forever will be nothing more than a canal. The river here is an engineer's dream, complete with 90-degree turns and beveled edges. Instead of deer, beavers and the other variety of wildlife which make the upper Sacramento River so special, instead you see nothing but the endless rock-lined shore and levees. After four hours of not seeing a living thing, Rucker suddenly ordered the canoe to the left shoreline.

"For a minute, I thought I actually saw a living critter," Rucker said. It turned out to be a Styrofoam float popping about.

Lining riverbanks with concrete rocks is known as "rip-rapping" and has been foisted off by the Army Corps of Engineers as "Riverbank Protection." They ought to rename it "Wildlife Destruction."

Like a person, a wild river changes from day to day, constantly cutting and modifying its course. Along the outside of bends, the water flows quickly, undermining and eroding the bank on that side, while deposits form a sandy or gravel beach along the inner bank. This is nature's way. And right there's the problem. Farmers plant orchards right to the river's edge and discover their trees suddenly falling into the river—the soil being eaten by the natural erosion. The river giveth and the river taketh away. So the Army Corps has stepped in, rip-rapping most of the river from Colusa to Sacramento.

Rip-rapping has a severe effect on fish life because it destroys the natural riparian vegetation which produces insects and other fish food. In addition, the large rocks and cement blocks provide shelter for such predators as squawfish, which prey on juvenile trout and salmon.

Trees and other vegetation "are discouraged" on rip-rap projects because the roots tend to break into the rocks and "cut the effectiveness of the structure," according to the Army Corps of Engineers.

We kept on, not a cheerful face among us, and near dusk, we arrived at Miller Park in Sacramento. Neil Babcock staggered out of the canoe and collapsed on the park's grass in an exhausted stupor, his eyes closing before he hit the ground.

"When this thing is over, I'm going to go on a 20-hour ordeal of standing up," said Babcock, before crumbling into unconsciousness.

When some folks conjure up a vision of a 400-mile canoe trip down the majestic Sacramento, they probably see some leisurely vacation joyride, the crew members sitting back with their feet up, quaffing cold beers. We learned that's just a fantasy. The best part was a sensation of becoming one with the river. The worst parts were the physical demands, incited by long days on the river in 100 degree-plus temperatures. The easy way out would have been to quit. But then we would have lost our bet with the ghosts of the Hudson Bay Company.

"We're gonna make it if it's the last damn thing I ever do," said Jeff Dickinson of Redding, looking like Jesse James, with a red bandanna covering his face to prevent the sun from blistering his skin any further.

With 200 miles of river left behind, a strong sense of unity had bonded us. One for all. All for one. Leading that spirit was Tom Ward—a stoic fellow who has the kind of battle-scarred past that brushes with the Twilight Zone. Ward was the *West Wind's* "bow man," which meant that he stood at the head of the canoe, spotting obstacles, determining direction and pacing the paddlers behind him. He never missed a stroke—and instead of collapsing at the end of the day, he would set up camp and engineer all cooking duties. This was a man of special fiber. It showed in everything he did, as if he were driven by something deep within, and his past helps explain why.

In another era, Tom Ward would be a national hero. But in this one, like most Vietnam veterans, he keeps his past locked inside. In Vietnam, Ward was a buck sergeant working in the Special Forces, a division which dealt primarily in hand-to-hand combat. The average range of fire was about 10 yards. "Yeah, I got shot up several times," Ward admitted after I pressed him about his past one evening. "Once, after I was shot, I literally sawed the enemy in half with my machine gun. It was him or me."

After leaving Vietnam, Ward wandered about the West, including taking a nine-month backpack trip on the Pacific Crest Trail, until he ran into Neil Rucker in Redding. Almost immediately, Ward was hired as manager of Rucker's canoe shop. And as the bow man aboard the *West Wind*, he led the way by example.

"I don't get tired," Ward said. "If I get some sleep, fine. If I don't, it doesn't bother me that much. If there's something to be done, I'd just as soon do it. If I just stay busy…it's easier for me that way."

He was an inspirational figure for the crew trying to match his strokes, a motley bunch if there ever was one. The crew was composed primarily of teachers, their family members and former students.

Neil Rucker, captain of the *West Wind*, had been a high school English and drama instructor for 17 years. "I picked people that I knew would stay with it despite anything we'd face," he said. His choices were:

Renee Rucker, Neil's daughter: "My dad is the most amazing man on earth. He can do anything. I know we'll make it because he's in charge."

Ann Powers, an educator who teaches students with reading disabilities: "I am determined to see all of the river, all the way to San Francisco. I don't fail at things. When I set out to do something, I do it."

Jeff Dickinson, a student: "This is the ultimate challenge. A friend of mine and I were going to try it on a wood raft, but Mr. Rucker said our chances of making it were one-in-a-thousand. 'Instead,' he said, 'come with me.'"

Tom Ward, bow man: "I don't admire my tenacity—it's stupid. The only thing keeping me going is that I'm scared to death of those sharks I've heard about in the Bay."

Terry Rucker, nephew of the captain, who spent four years in the Navy as a quartermaster: "This experience is like climbing a mountain; not every step is easy. You do it because it's there—and the adventure waits for you."

Clark Tuthill, a high school history teacher: "I suggest any politician who cares about the integrity of the river should take a trip down this river and see it for himself. It's obvious man's manipulation has damaged the environment."

Mark Tuthill, a youngster who celebrated his 13th birthday on the second day of the trip: "It's been a lot tougher than I expected but I can stand up to it."

Neil Babcock, a high school art teacher: "Hey, it suddenly hit me that San Francisco is a long, long ways away. There are a lot of kinds of trips and this is one of the other kinds."

Curt Babcock, Neil's son: "Man, I tell you this, I've never been on anything like this before."

Bill Sundahl, a research technician for Pacific Southeast Experimentation Center: "If we don't make it, there will a darn good reason."

Steve Scoggins, a student: "It has been difficult, but we're getting something out of this that is very special."

Katy Raddatz, a photographer for the *San Francisco Examiner:* "We'll make it because of our captain and the morale of the crew. I've never doubted Neil (Rucker) from the moment I met him."

From Colusa to Sacramento was the first psychological test of the crew—32 hours of paddling in 36 hours, through what was nothing more than an irrigation canal, could have triggered the depths of depression for anyone aboard. But the crew responded by turning inward, to each other.

Befuddled strangers would strain their eyes, seemingly in shock. Trains, trucks and cars would blast their horns to celebrate our arrival. Even coarsened old souls behind television cameras would arch their eyebrows as they spotted the huge canoe being paddled down the river.

"So, you're the famous Redding Pioneers, eh?" they would ask.

A Redding Pioneer? What's that?

"You," they would answer, showing us newspaper stories detailing our voyage to Fisherman's Wharf. Thanks for telling us.

Unknown to us, the news media had nicknamed us—and that label became our trademark everywhere. At Miller Park in Sacramento, the "Redding Pioneers" were even presented with a key to the city by the mayor. It was a kind gesture, similar in spirit to how most folks reacted to a motley crew of mugwumps—though specific responses varied wildly, from good-natured cheer to utter disbelief to derision.

Some strangers' tales preceded our arrival at the frequent marinas and small towns along the old Sacramento River. By watching us, it was as if some folks had received a one-way trip to Fantasyland.

At grocery stores and rest stops along the river, several mystifying rumors kept turning up.

We heard that we "flipped over a boulder and lost all of our gear near Los Molinos." At one store, this tale was told to me twice—one time further enhanced by an account of our captain Neil Rucker making a heroic "rescue of one of our female paddlers lost in a rapid." Others reported that we "were secretly using a small engine when nobody was looking" and that we "were staying at hotels along the way and loading up on milk shakes and hamburgers." They heeded the old joke: Never let the facts get in the way of a good story.

The media wasn't completely truthful either. Television, radio and newspaper accounts from Redding to Sacramento reported that the "Redding Pioneers" were en route on an incredible "600-mile voyage." If Rucker planned on ordering us back up the river for another 200 miles, well, that would have triggered a mutiny and one skipper was going to walk the plank.

When people spotted us on the river, the onlookers would gather on the banks and stare in awe at the strange craft and the paddles dipping in unison. Inevitably, some wise guy would shout: "Stroke! Stroke! Stroke!"—timing his shouts perfectly with each dip of the paddle.

After a week of this, all of us were ready to stroke our paddles right down a few throats. All in fun, of course. Heh, heh, heh. In Sacramento, a huge semi-truck crossed above us on a bridge at 50 miles per hour, blasted his horn three times and then yelled out of his window the hated words: "Stroke! Stroke! Stroke!"

We gave him a paddle salute.

Our tortoise-like speed drew remarks, especially from folks at the thousand or so marinas along the river, all which posted the sign: "5 m.p.h. speed limit, watch your wake." These restrictions are to prevent high-speed boats from making the river look like the water in a washing machine, not for canoes traveling at four miles per hour. But it never failed. Some guy would come running down the ramp with a silly grin, wave at us and shout, "Hey, watch your wake. Yuk, yuk, yuk." Then for good measure he'd yell, "Stroke! Stroke! Stroke!"

For the onlookers who had no conception of what was our chosen task, puzzled lines would cross their faces and then they would ask, in order, what became known as The Questions: 1. "Where are you from?" 2. "Where are you going?" 3. "How big is the canoe?" 4. "Are you kidding?" 5. "Are you nuts?"

These questions became so predictable that Terry Rucker planned on making a banner by mounting a sheet between a pair of oars, then raising it to every passerby. Its contents would be simple: 1. "From Redding." 2. "To San Francisco." 3. "36-feet, eight inches." 4. "No, we're not kidding." 5. "Yes."

A sunrise on the Sacramento River is a reminder of the awesome power of nature. That fireball in the sky rises over the hills to the east, sending oranges and yellows across the water—and you realize that in a canoe you are at nature's whim, at the mercy of unpredictable forces. So far we had been lucky, despite temperatures as high as 120 degrees. From Redding on past Sacramento, a gentle breeze was at our backs, helping us along downstream. The crew spoke rarely of this good fortune, in fear that it might evaporate at any mention of it. Finally, our captain could no longer hold the words.

"Hell, let's take advantage of this wind while we have it," shouted Neil Rucker. "The Voyageurs would have." He instructed the rigging of a crude sail—a ground tarp tied between a pair of oars.

Immediately it filled out and pulled us along at three miles per hour, like a gift from heaven. I dropped my paddle and was asleep within 20 seconds. Terrible fate that it might be, I dreamed, yes, of paddling. But with a jolt I was awakened, and saw the look of apprehension in the eyes of every crew member.

While asleep, that fickle wind had switched on us, and it was now a devil blowing right in our face, as if taunting us. The paddles returned to the water, but it felt like we were paddling in maple syrup. With Suisun Bay, Carquinez Strait, San Pablo and San Francisco Bays looming ahead, the final 100 miles were foreboding. I remembered what Ken Castle said: "It can be hell out there."

It was silent for a long time, as if each member of the crew was quietly summoning the determination to keep on in the face of this wind. It wasn't until later that Bill Sundahl, a quiet and profound man, made public one of the few thoughts he uttered the entire week.

"This old sea and wind gives quarter to no one," he said.

For the first time, we finally realized just how difficult this voyage could become.

Every one of us was ragged, dirty and cursing the wind blowing in our faces. That, along with an incoming tide, cut our speed to a tortoise-like two miles per hour. The strain was showing in our faces. Even Terry Rucker, who has an unique spark about him, had his spirits dulled. Yet we all knew that our captain might demand that we paddle on into the night in order to catch a helpful outgoing tide. The Carquinez Strait, a treacherous stretch of water in a wind, seemed just around the bend.

"When we reach Carquinez Strait, we'll find out if Nature's on our side," I said privately to Rucker. "Our fate is in her hands."

In preparation for the last 80 miles, our crew had done an immense amount of fact finding and soul searching. Regardless, we actually had very little to say about the rest of the trip.

"Nature will decide," I thought to myself as I drifted off to sleep.

It's 3:30 a.m., it's dreary, dark and windy and it's a good time to be in bed, snoozing away, right? Then why is somebody grabbing my foot to wake me up? Because it's time to paddle. "C'mon Rip Van Winkle, it's time to get up and go," ordered Captain Bligh.

But after loading the canoe in darkness, the prospects for the day ahead looked bleak. We had hoped to beat the Delta's summer winds by getting an early start, then later catching an outgoing tide through the dreaded Carquinez Strait. We were wrong on both counts. In the early morning blackness, that foul wind was again blowing in our faces, daring us to quit. With an empty stomach and tired eyes, I tried to put my body on automatic paddle, but it kept trying to switch to automatic sleep. Our speed was about two or three miles per hour—too slow to reach the Carquinez Strait by that afternoon's outgoing tide.

For the first time, some crew members had become cranky, critical of a few folk's paddling styles. That devil of divisiveness was creeping aboard. The gripes started surfacing. "This sure ain't what I had in mind and it sucks," said Clark Tuthill. "Whatever happened to the beauty and whitewater of the north country?" We had left it behind long ago.

With Fisherman's Wharf beckoning some 50 miles away, we'd had no injuries, no serious arguments. But now there were tight faces and few smiles, an undercurrent of discontent. I wondered if the Voyageurs bickered over headwinds.

The sunrise was a spectacle as we passed Decker Island, hues of pink spanning a hundred miles on the horizon. It should have been an awe-inspiring event. Instead, I passed out into an unconscious stupor for 20 minutes, and I think I just kept stroking away all the while. The wind blew in our faces at 20 knots.

At 9 a.m., after struggling against that hated headwind for five tedious hours, the paddling slowly eased near Port Chicago in Suisun Bay, where members of the U.S. Navy stopped loading bombs to eye our canoe. They couldn't believe what we were doing and considering the wind, neither could we. But, suddenly, as if nature had thrown a giant master switch, the paddling pain was eased by a strong outgoing tide. It was an answer to 14 silent prayers. The big canoe cut through the wind, hustling along Suisun Bay at three miles per hour as people along the shoreline gawked.

But at 2 p.m., the tide had turned against us again, joining the gale headwind, making each stroke an exercise in futility. We were forced to dock in the marina, and we staggered into Martinez.

"We're not going anywhere in that wind and tide," Captain Rucker told us. "We'll just have to wait it out." Then he set his jaw. "But one way or another, we're gonna get through Carquinez Strait tonight."

The Carquinez Strait is a narrow, 10-mile water-filled canyon which connects San Pablo and Suisun Bays. Sea captains talk of its dangers in mythic terms. Every summer, the combination of a high-pressure system and moderate temperatures off the Pacific Coast and a low-pressure system and high temperatures in the Central Valley cause afternoon westerly winds to gust through the Carquinez Strait. It's nature's way of balancing the pressure systems. But it can cause nautical havoc.

On the Carquinez Bridge, these blasts of wind can send cars reeling from lane to lane and have caused some motorcyclists to consider adding training wheels. For the boaters below, it can be a watery hell. Small craft are tossed about like soap bubbles in a breeze. On those huge tanker ships that fill up at the Pittsburg oil refineries, more hats have probably been blown off than at any other place in the world.

In a canoe, of all things, it can be the end. "I'd advise you folks to get some rest while you have the chance," our captain said. "We'll be back on the water before nightfall."

By quitting for a while, we had remained true to the historical practices of the real Voyageurs. Although they would persevere through freezing cold and violent squalls, the Voyageurs would call it quits when faced with hurricane-like headwinds. They would recoup their pride in the near-religious partaking of grog. So in order to continue on the historic path of our predecessors, I walked into Bill's Bait in Martinez and bought a six-pack.

Five hours later, we were back at it, the paddles rhythmically dipping into the water. The gale wind had faded along with the day, Neptune now permitting our passage across the strait in the early evening. We reached the headlands of Benicia in only two hours, ready for a solid night's rest before challenging the final leg of the trip—San Pablo and San Francisco Bays.

Cement doesn't make the best bed, but after the past week, nobody was griping. The wind and tide forced us to overnight at Benicia State "Park," which consisted of a parking lot and a locked restroom. A roadway was the best place we could find to throw our sleeping bags for the night. It wasn't lonely. After all, we had the company of football-sized rats which were dodging in and out of the rocks. Life can still be exciting here in the 20th century.

At the park in Benicia, we were astounded that there was not one piece of soft ground, only concrete and rocks. But for Terry Rucker, it didn't make any difference.

"I slept like a rock," he said the next morning.

Only one day and 22 miles stood in the way of completing our 400-mile voyage from Redding to Fisherman's Wharf. But whatever excitement the last day held, it was tempered by the potential terror of becoming fodder for one of the nine-foot, 300-pound sharks which roam the waters near Alcatraz.

"The only thing keeping me in the boat is that I'm scared to death of those sharks in the Bay," said the otherwise fearless Tom Ward.

With a quick flip from one of the sea's mighty arms, the canoe could be scooped up in a flash and dumped into the briny blue of the Bay, while Neptune, the Sea God, laughed at our folly. After having staggered through Carquinez Strait, our remaining doubts keyed on the reports of the 20-knot winds which had busted east through the Golden Gate. We were later told that the Bay looked like a huge washing machine, complete with foaming whitecaps.

Captain Neil Rucker stretched out on the concrete, had a draw from his pipe and took a skeptical look at the Carquinez Strait. "Somehow we made it through that thing," he said.

We awoke early. With no wind and an outgoing tide, we whistled through San Pablo Bay, around Point Pinole and under the Richmond Bridge. So far, so good. But even going fast in a canoe is quite slow by modern standards. At 2 p.m., we reached Angel Island in San Francisco Bay and landed. Three of us climbed the ridge to see what lay ahead.

Fisherman's Wharf lay just two miles away for the 14 Voyageurs and the 37-foot canoe *West Wind*. But it didn't look like we were going to make it.

From our perch atop the ridge, we could see whitecaps as high as our canoe, a crushing sight. The seas were pushed by a 20-knot headwind and a strong incoming tide. The only signs in our favor were our determination to succeed and the nearby Coast Guard boat waiting to pick up any bodies that might be floating about the Bay shortly.

The view from Angel Island is one of the most spectacular anywhere—that golden span at the gateway to the Bay…Alcatraz and the towering high rises of the City sitting just over yonder…southward, the Bay Bridge stretching out to the banks of Treasure Island. But three Voyageurs took in this spectacle in grim silence. That hideous wind from the west brought nothing but disdain.

Was this the stopper? Could we reach Fisherman's Wharf?

"Let's be honest about it. There's a good chance we won't be able to make it," said Voyageur Clark Tuthill.

We watched as two men in a 17-foot canoe, who had come out to greet us, tried the crossing and flipped over. The Coast Guard quickly rescued the ejected occupants. Our attempt was next.

The final crossing would be like reaching for the clouds. Terry Rucker was unsure of our chances of success. For the first time in a week, the crew was seriously divided.

Captain Neil Rucker settled our differences with a concise

speech. "We'll go out and see what it's like and try to make it to Alcatraz," he said. "If it looks like bad news, we'll turn around and try to come back. That Coast Guard boat is there if anything goes wrong."

As we paddled out from Angel Island, saltwater splashed over the canoe and slapped our faces, as if nature was taunting us to quit. But we paddled on. Terry Rucker, sitting directly in front of me, believed he saw a shark hovering just to our left.

We ripped at the water with our paddles, gaining perhaps a foot—then losing that foot against the incoming tide when we raised our paddles for the next stroke. For 10 minutes, we continued the futility, trying to make it to Alcatraz for a rest stop.

"We're not making any ground at all!" our captain barked. "Switch course for the Wharf. Put the wood in the water and stroke like you mean it."

So this would be it. Either we have what it takes or we don't. This final leg turned into a silent vigil, us against the sea. The paddles windmilled through the water, little whirlpools trailing behind our strokes. After 15 minutes, it appeared we had gained some distance, however minuscule. Regardless, it was a key sign. If we had to turn back now, our trip would have been shattered.

I glanced behind at Neil Rucker, his scruffy week's growth of beard speckled with sparkling water droplets. This was the man who had sweated blood designing and building this canoe, and now he had personally guided it past untold obstacles for hundreds of miles. That wharf, looming just a few thousand yards away, was like the Promised Land.

Our eyes locked. "We're gonna make it, my friend," he said. We had paddled side by side for the entire distance.

The crew sensed the victory. The once-frantic strokes settled into a powerful rhythm, each biting the Bay, turning back the water as we claimed the prize. That prize is the experience. No amount of words or pictures can make you feel it.

We were stroking evenly now, in perfect harmony again, and as we slid into a berth at the Wharf, an old wise song rang in the back of my mind:

The way that you wander
Is the way that you choose.
And the day that you tarry
Is the day that you lose.

For information on canoeing and rafting on the Sacramento River, call or write Rent-a-Raft, 2515 Park Marina, Redding, CA 96001; (916) 246-8388.

For information on rafting only, call Turtle River Rafting at (800) 726-3223, or call California River Outfitters at (800) 552-3625 for a directory of all rafting companies that run rafting trips in California.

Tom holds his prize catch: a 42-pound, 52-inch Mackinaw trout

Hooking a
42-POUNDER

and Other Canadian Fishing Tales

❖

Back in the early 1960s, a little kid stole away to bed with a copy of *Field & Stream* and a flashlight. When all the lights in the house went out, the flashlight flicked on and the back pages of the magazine flipped open.

A picture in a small advertisement for Great Bear Lake seemed unbelievable. It was just a man holding a trout, but this trout was about four feet long and sure didn't look like any trout this kid had ever seen. That faint picture from the dying beam of the flashlight was like a branding iron on the back of that kid's mind. Twenty-five years later, he still remembered it.

That kid was me. Then one day at the San Francisco Sports & Boat Show, I was walking down an aisle when the sign "Great Bear Lake" reached out and grabbed me like a giant squid putting his clamps on a whale. Dreams don't come cheap, I learned. For a few thousand bucks, the man said, you can get on a jet and be fishing out of Trophy Lodge for giant trout in the Arctic the next evening.

My practical, rational mind started warring with my impractical, passionate heart. "Logic gives you what you need, but passion gives you what you crave," I told myself, trying to rationalize it. "That is why you have a heart." Life isn't a dress rehearsal, right? A few days later, the obvious hit me: I figured out that I just wanted a chance to catch some of those giant trout.

The Arctic? In August, the tundra is filled with caribou, moose and musk-ox, not snow. The breeze on the lake is cool, but not biting. The only bites are on the end of your fishing line, not on your ankles from mosquitoes.

The months passed quickly, then suddenly summer came and off I went—flying thousands of miles north to the Arctic Circle, to Great Bear Lake in Canada's Northwest Territories. In the first four days at Great Bear Lake, I caught and released about 300 fish. What? Three hundred fish? The stuff of a dream lost and found again.

Mackinaw trout ranging from 5 to 10 pounds would attack a spoon trolled just five- to eight-feet deep. Then in a cove, we hooked Arctic grayling, 14- to 22-inchers, on 25 consecutive casts, using a fly rod and spinning outfits. My largest missed the world record by three ounces.

Want more? Near the mouth of a feeder stream, my guide rigged a Labatt's Blue beer can with a treble hook, cast it out, and caught big northern pike on six of 10 casts. Hey, the fish here bite similar to the way you take your first bite of a cheeseburger after three weeks in the mountains.

"Now we look for the monsters," said my guide, Trevor Slaymaker, a rugged soul who works in the wilderness year round.

Great Bear Lake is located practically on top of the world in the Northwest Territories, where winter spans from mid-October to June, when the lake freezes 10 feet thick. That gives the fish just 10 weeks to feed, 10 weeks to gorge on anything that moves before another 42 weeks of winter shuts them down. They don't waste much time when they get the chance to eat. You cast, the fish bite.

Trophy Lodge, my "base camp," is set in isolation amid a stark kind of wild beauty. There isn't another lodge within 200 miles. Fragile grasses, wildflowers and old, scrawny pines cover the tundra. It sits less than a mile from where world-record trout have been caught. The lake is so huge, covering more than 12,000 square miles, yet fished so lightly, that the giant trout, grayling and pike have little fear of an angler's bag of magic. It will always remain that way. Canadian authorities permit fishermen to take only two fish—

one over 28 inches, one under—so virtually all the fish are returned to the lake.

The bonus is that the fish are no deeper than 10 or 15 feet in the lake, since the oxygen content becomes minimal any deeper. That factor allows anglers to use light tackle for maximum excitement, since you don't have to power lift fish up from the depths. In the shallows, the fish head off in the only direction available—away— for thumb-burning, line-stripping runs. You lose a fish because of the light tackle? No problem. Cast again and hook another one.

The blip-blip from the depth finder told my guide that fish were beneath the boat.

"That's not what we're looking for," Trevor said. I knew exactly what he meant.

We were looking for what Canadians call "hogs," a giant lake trout, the kind that makes other trout look like guppies. Lake Tahoe has Mackinaw trout and the state record is 37 pounds, six ounces. But at Tahoe, these trout average just four or five pounds and live at a depth of 250 feet. At Great Bear, they're right under your boat. But even at Great Bear, there are secret spots where the unimaginable is possible.

To reach such a spot, Trevor Slaymaker and I took off at 4 p.m., then cruised at top speed until the sun went down at midnight, when we set up a wilderness camp on shore. At sunrise, about 3:30 a.m., we took off again, arriving six hours later at a remote bay few know of. In the bay, we began probing the lake bottom with the depth finder, searching for habitat that might hold giant trout. Eventually, we discovered an area where the bottom was just eight feet deep, yet cut by a 15-foot deep trough, about 30 feet wide. Finally. It seemed perfect.

I clipped on a chartreuse-colored Huskie-Devil spoon, a five-inch metal lure, and cast it behind the boat. Slowly we worked up and down the underwater trough. All was quiet and tense. We trolled and waited.

My mind started drifting. I remembered the old days when, as a kid, I first spotted that magazine ad, and how I wore out the flashlight batteries looking at it. I was in Dreamland when my rod tip was practically ripped into the water. Automatically, I set the hook and felt this remarkable surge on the line.

"A hog! A hog!" shouted Trevor.

The fish spun off 80 more yards of line; with only 150 yards of 10-pound test on my reel, there wasn't much more to spare.

The big trout went down, across, circled, crossed under the boat, then off again. I was living the dream. A half hour later, we peered down through the crystal clear waters and suddenly spotted the fish. It looked as big as the one in that old magazine ad. After we landed it, I just sat there, kind of stunned, staring at it.

The next morning, it was time to leave. I packed slowly and hiked out to the dirt "airport" runway near the lodge. I was the last in line to board the prop jet, our ticket out of the Arctic frontier. While walking up the steps of the plane, I stopped and turned, catching the eyes of three guides there to see us off.

"How big was that beaut you caught, mate?" asked a guide.

"Hard to believe," I answered. "Forty-two pounds, 52 inches long. Also got a 38, 30 and 25 the same day and several other big ones, threw them back. Let me tell you, it's tough to get on this plane. I admit I don't really feel like going back."

"Then stay," said Trevor, my guide. "Stay here and be a guide with us."

"Sure," said another. "Join us."

I took a few more steps up the ladder to the prop jet. I turned and looked at the three guides for 10 seconds, maybe more, then continued onward. Those last few steps up the ladder and into the plane were some of the steepest I've ever climbed.

When you stand on the shoreline of Nimpo Lake at night, it sounds like somebody is throwing bricks in the lake. But they aren't bricks. They are rainbow trout jumping five to eight feet in the air, then landing with a splash that can be heard for a mile in the still Canadian night.

Later, as you try to sleep in a lakeside cabin, the sound of the giant splashes can keep you awake for hours. As you lay there in bed listening, you will start imagining the size of these jumping trout. But it won't be long—tomorrow—before you discover their size on the end of your fishing line.

What you find is that fighting these fish is like lassoing a Hells Angel on his Harley and trying to pull him in with your bare hands. They average 16 to 17 inches. Twenty-inchers are common, and with a little luck and a week of fishing, you'll connect with a 24- to 26-inch mountain-bred rainbow trout that goes 5 to 8 pounds and is as strong as Poseidon's pet Kraken.

This is the best western Canada can offer. Nimpo Lake is your headquarters, located 300 air miles (500 by car) northwest of Vancouver, B.C., set on the edge of the glacier-cut Coast Mountain Range. Here you get the best rainbow trout fishing for the price in the Western Hemisphere.

Lodges in Alaska offering a comparable adventure set the price at $2,500 to $3,500 for a week. Rainbow Lodge at Nimpo provides a cabin, all meals, boats and motors, and three fly-out fishing trips for $850 a week. The lodge capacity is only 10 and there are usually just four to six people visiting because not many people know about it. When I heard this, I plunked down my check almost as fast as the trout bite.

And they can bite like dogs. Between longtime fishing companion Ed "The Dunk" Dunckel and myself, we caught 20 to 25 trout in two days, and about 70 for the trip. In one 20-minute stretch, we landed trout that measured 19, 21 and 24 inches, the latter weighing five-and-a-half pounds.

When they strike, it feels like a bear grabbing you by the arm. If you are new to fishing, you will know you are getting a bite when you practically get pulled into the lake. We saw one fellow sitting in his boat, drinking a cup of coffee, his fishing rod resting unattended against the boat rail. Suddenly, a big trout hit so hard that the power of it flipped his rod into the lake, where it disappeared into the depths. It happened so fast the guy couldn't believe it. He took a long drink of coffee, then just stared at the lake for about fifteen minutes.

But in Canada you are apt to see a lot of things you have never before imagined. You see bald eagles every day, many of them. One evening, we saw an osprey make a dive into the lake, grab a trout, then go flying off without missing a wingbeat. Suddenly, a huge bald eagle came screaming down from above and blitzed the osprey, forcing it to drop the trout. The eagle then swooped down, and while flying upside down, caught the trout in its talons, righted itself and flapped off. You see it and you still can't quite believe it.

But that's how it is. You see even more during the fly-out trips, with 60 lakes and the Dean River within 45 minutes of flight time. The float planes provide personalized air tours, with a chance to see moose, mountain goats and caribou, and a guarantee to see Hunlen Falls. This is a waterfall that looks like it drops off the edge of the earth—1,200 feet of water in all with 900 feet of free fall. On our visit, we circled the waterfall twice in the small plane, then executed a banking, diving turn over the falls, plunging 500 feet adjacent to cascading water in a granite canyon, before pulling the plane out of the dive and over the tree tops.

"Nothing to be scared of," the pilot said with a laugh. "We're not even tipped at 90 degrees."

This kind of excitement runs through most elements of the trip. But because you are freed from distractions and pressures, from phone calls, loose ends and heavy traffic, your inner coil will start to unwind, no matter how tightly wound from months of work. You will realize it if the fishing slows.

We had one zilch of a day when we caught just one trout apiece. The Dunk just laughed. "You weren't relaxed enough when you were catching all those big fish yesterday," he said. "They stopped biting so you will remember you're supposed to be on vacation. So sit there and do nothing for a change."

The last day of the trip, we landed at Hotnarko Lake, about a 20-minute flight, then climbed in an aluminum boat and motored off in search of 10-pound rainbow trout.

Many flies and lures can entice strikes, but what works best are black or gray wooly worm flies, black or pink No. 30 or 50 Hot Shots, and fluorescent red F-6 Flatfish. Some people troll with small sets of flashers as attractors. If you go, fill up your tackle box with all of them. Then troll the underwater ledges, skirting the giant submerged boulders. Another trick is to work where you see bubbles on the lake surface; the bubbles are the result of one of those jumping trout landing like a falling brick.

We were working the bubbles when a trout struck so hard that the Dunk's rod tip got jerked in the water. Zip, zip, zip—you could hear the line zipping off his level-wind reel.

Then 50 yards away, this huge tail cut the surface of the lake.

"Look at that tail!" Dunckel shouted. "It must be eight inches across!"

An instant later, there was a huge swirl, and the line went limp. The line had been broken. "He's gone," Dunckel said. "The biggest trout of my life and he's gone."

That evening, as we left by plane, Dunckel looked down on the lake and smiled.

"What the heck, that's okay," he said, remembering the giant trout. "That gives me something to come back for."

And you bet we will.

The Cariboo is a rugged land of wildlife and trees, bald eagles and big fish, grizzly bears and legends. It covers a swath of British Columbia, Canada, where people live for the pure exhilaration of the outdoors. It was here where the biggest rainbow trout I'd ever seen broke my friend Ed Dunckel's 10-pound test line and vanished deep into the lake. As time went by, that image of the line snapping and the trout disappearing kept replaying itself in my mind. For a fisherman, that was the darkest kind of torture.

There was only one antidote: To return! And after a year's wait, we did. We found ourselves at Hotnarko Lake, set deep in the Cariboo, hoping for a rematch with the big one that got away.

A small boat had been stashed in the trees at the lake, and it didn't take long to get it turned over, our gear stowed, and the small motor running. My dad, Robert Sr., had joined us for the trip. He picked through the tackle box and selected a wooly worm fly.

"That's the one he wants," he said. "Pure black. He's too smart for anything else."

You become a believer when one of these trout strikes. While we were trolling, I was tying a new leader and had my rod propped up against my leg, when suddenly the rod went shooting the length of the boat. The only thing that kept it from flying into the lake was the reel ramming against the boat's stern. It had been yanked by the bite of a trout. That fish turned out to be a 22-inch rainbow trout, the first fish we kept, placing it on the metal stringer. But get this: A half-hour later, we went to take a look at the trout, and it was gone. The metal stringer had been broken off.

Back at the lodge, nobody quite believed this tale. Then Colleen Haavlik, co-owner of the lodge, said the exact same thing had been reported several times before. "Guys have lost some beautiful trout with those metal stringers," she said. "They practically want to cry when it happens. That's why we put fish boxes in the boats. The big trout can break those metal stringers right off."

This is big country and you see it first-hand on the fly-out trips. The plane takes off from Nimpo Lake at 3,600 feet, and after gaining 500 feet, you can see lodgepole pine forests stretching for miles, interspersed by untouched lakes, ponds and streams. Mountains with 13,000-foot glacial-cut peaks provide the background.

But we were there for big fish, not the views, and off we went. The float plane settled on Hotnarko Lake, the scene of the crime where Ed Dunckel had lost that huge trout the previous year. Dunckel was in a nearby boat with his son, Alan.

"A lady caught an eight-pounder there last week," said Richard Haavlik. "I know that's not as big as the one you guys lost last year, but it gives you an idea of what's biting."

The water was so clear that you could see giant submerged boulders and also where the bottom dropped off in underwater shelves. We would troll or cast along these areas, and in a week we caught more than 75 trout and had a top day of 25 trout, virtually all 15- to 20-inchers, some bigger.

"This is the best fishing I've ever had," my dad said. But last year's big one that got away continued to elude us.

Just then, I raised my binoculars to my eyes to get a look at the other boat on the lake. As the image came into focus, I spotted Ed Dunckel, with his rod bent in a complete half circle around the boat. At one point, Alan raised the net, and there was a bowling-ball sized splash on the surface, then the fish went deep again. Five minutes later, Alan lowered the net, but the fish disappeared again.

From their expressions, it looked like they had the big one that got away. Then a moment later, the fish was suddenly in the net, in the boat—they had caught it.

It was late in the day, and just then, the float plane buzzed overhead, returning to pick us up. Suddenly, both my dad and I hooked up, a double-header, 20- and 18-inchers.

At the plane, we got a close look at Dunckel's big trout: Twenty-five inches with the brightest red stripe you've ever seen running down its side.

"It's a beauty," Dunckel said. Then a few minutes later, he added with a grin, "Well, this is a big one, but he isn't last year's big one that got away. I'll be back for him. You can count on that."

Wild, native wonder covers much of the backcountry of western Canada, but there's one giant chunk of land in the Rockies that is unlike any other in the world.

Winding its way around glaciers and tree-filled mountains is a 75-mile canoe loop linked by 13 lakes, six rivers and seven portages. It is called the Bowron Lake Provincial Park, but to people who have been here, it is known better as one of the great wilderness adventures in the Western Hemisphere.

It is a demanding trip, but nowhere as difficult as wilderness backpacking up long, high-altitude grades. Because you use a canoe, not a backpack, you don't have to thump your way around the mountains with 55 pounds on your back. You put your gear in the boat, and the only sounds you hear are of paddles dipping in quiet water, along with the occasional splashes of jumping trout.

When I first plunked my canoe into little Kibbee Lake, it was the start of an adventure I had waited years to undertake. A sense of mystery hung in the air with those first few paddle strokes. As long as you're on the water, it's a feeling that stays with you. The water was like a mirror, with little whirlpools from each paddle stroke trailing behind the boat as we forged into the Canadian wilderness.

You're going where nobody has ever walked. Look over there! A moose and its baby are swimming across the lake. Hey! The trout are jumping again. The lake is perfectly calm, with glaciers reflecting off the lake's surface.

Most people take 11 or 12 days for the entire loop circuit, though it can be done more quickly with longer days at the paddles. My partner Terry Dunckel and I scheduled five days for the trip. Because the Bowron Lake circuit has become known around the world, reservations are now required for a departure slot, and you can plan on seeing other canoeists on the route. We met people from Palo Alto, Germany and Switzerland. If another boat gets a 300-yard lead on you, it can be irritating to have to look at them

Opposite: The one that didn't get away: Ed Dunckel and his 25-inch trout

ahead of you all day. We avoided that by not letting anyone get
ahead of us, waiting a while if they did.

The trip started with a rough portage, over a mile, and then after
the paddle across Kibbee Lake, yet another even rougher portage up
and over a hill. In the first three portages, when you put your canoe
yoke on your shoulders and walk to the next lake, you can feel like
Samson carrying the world on his shoulders. My canoe weighed 79

pounds, and I wouldn't have wanted to carry another ounce.

The other variables are the weather and the mosquitoes. Clouds can form and dump a thundershower at any time, but from mid-July to mid-August the region gets more sun than at any time of the year. However, that's also when the mosquitoes fly in massive squadrons. We chose late August, risking a chance at more rain, but definitely avoiding the mosquitoes. But rain? It rained so hard, with drops so large, that it looked like the raindrops were bouncing several inches off the lake surface. It started to fill the canoe, and twice we had to unpack the boat and drain it. When our camp stove blew up, forcing us to build campfires each night for cooking, it could have been a disaster. Instead, it was just more adventure, since the Canadian Park Service provides cut rounds at each camp. With an ax, the inside of those rounds can furnish dry firewood.

And the fishing? Heh, heh, heh. Oh yeah, the fishing. Here's a secret that is dynamite in British Columbia: Simply paddle along the shoreline, trailing a wooly worm fly without any weight. Nothing to it. Just tie a No. 12 olive green wooly worm fly directly to your line. That's it. That will get you dinner.

Another secret is not to worry about if you've "got enough time" to finish the 75-mile trip. That can be a terrible pressure for many, causing them to rush through the first half of the circuit. In fact, it is the first three lakes—Kibbee, Indianpoint and giant Isaac Lake—that provide the best views, paddling and fishing by far. At Isaac Lake, the wind died, the clouds disappeared, and we were framed perfectly on the huge, still lake by glaciers. Nothing could disturb the scene's tranquility. Even a short visit by a momma bear and two cubs at camp passed without a hint of a problem.

By the time you've reached the halfway point, you will have developed a strong paddling stroke. Your canoe pace will have quickened but will require less effort. The portages become short, and a few easy rivers send you downstream without a stroke being made. The rivers are a pleasure, gliding along, heaven-sent after so much effort to reach the midpoint of the circuit.

The rivers are Class I, beginner level, so they are nothing to worry about as long as you practice a minimum of caution. To ensure safe river paddling, the rangers show you a 10-minute film about safety techniques before you set off.

So the rivers are enjoyable, coming after a few long days at the paddle. The exception is one short stretch where the stream is too shallow for paddling. Here you must get out, and with ropes extending from each end of the canoe, guide your boat. It is called "lining," and it can be a frustrating experience for newcomers without hip waders who don't want to get wet.

A friend of mine, Arman Klein, has completed the Bowron Lake Loop eight times, including a first visit in 1965. He keeps going back.

"This is God's country," Klein told me as we compared photos. "There's a holistic quality about doing this trip. It's the only trip of this nature that completes itself, start to finish. In a way, that is what life is supposed to be about."

My trip had one treacherous moment. Near the end of the circuit, the weather turned bad again, with high wind and driving rain. We guided the canoe downriver, pausing to enjoy a long flight of geese, then found ourselves poured by the river into an angry Bowron Lake. Big swells, white caps and a howling wind battered us. At times water poured over the gunwales. We kept perfectly vertical to the waves to keep from broaching, digging in with the paddles in deep, fast strokes, and in a half hour of a tense yet frenetic attack, we made it to shore. Safe. The trip was all but over.

Later, loading the canoe and gear into my rig, I noticed that a strange calm had come over me. Suddenly, I had learned how to listen. Instead of feeling impatient and irritable, I felt serene and tolerant. My hair-trigger had been diffused. Without even realizing it as it happened, paddling with a partner in the Canadian wilderness had freed me from every care. It is one of the best lessons I've ever been taught of the calming power of the wild outdoors.

Opposite: A peaceful moment on the Bowron Lake Loop.

It was the last week of August and already the aspen were turning color in the Chilcotin wilderness, three weeks early. Woodsmen say that's why the trout were so hungry.

"The trout know it's going to be an early winter, so they're trying to eat all they can now before it hits and takes over," said my dad, Bob Stienstra, Sr.

He glanced across Petry Lake, and right then a big trout jumped about 100 yards from the boat. A moment later, another one shot up, this time closer and higher. "There are so many jumping trout that it's like watching shooting stars," he said with a laugh, a winner's laugh.

That day we caught about 30 rainbow trout ranging from 16 to 21 inches, lost a few monsters, at least five-pounders, and kept eight for the smoker. These big trout strike with abandon, so hard that they can sprain your wrist if you're not ready for them. Then, when they're hooked, they jump like they're trying to touch the moon. When first brought near the boat, they turn around and blast off for never-never land as if you had poked them with an icepick.

For father and son, no matter what age, this is an exhilaration that can be shared on equal terms. A big trout can bridge any gap.

That was what inspired this trip to the wildlands of Canada. You see, just six months before, the late Jim Siegle, owner of a sport shop, told me he had cancer. If there was one thing he wished he could still do, he told me, it was to go fishing someplace special with his dad. "Now I can't do that," he said. "I missed my chance." It was the only time I ever saw tears in his eyes.

At Jim's funeral, I remembered those words so clearly, and then realized that I've never had any better friends and inspirations than my own mom and dad. When I was just a youngster, my dad taught me how to tie a knot and how to bait a hook, and he was right there with his arm around me when I caught my first fish and I was afraid it was going to pull me into the water. Later, when I was 13, I remember making a deal with him that I would never take drugs and that he would always take me fishing. We shook hands on it.

No times were more magical than those childhood summers, when everything was new and wonderful to a wild little kid, fixated by the unknowns of the great outdoors. After Jim died, I began picturing ways to recapture that magic, and then booked a trip with my dad to Rainbow Lodge at Nimpo Lake. I made the reservations and left a deposit. The time arrived, and we were flying across the Chilcotin in remote western British Columbia, landing on Petry Lake. In 15 minutes the plane was off and we were alone in a small boat, the lake so calm that the surrounding lodgepole pine forest and cobalt blue sky were mirrored perfectly on its surface.

"Ah-hoo!" I shouted, and the hoot echoed into a canyon and back across the lake as if penetrating the walls of time. I remember doing the same thing for the first time when I was 10 years old.

"Hooo-ah!" came the return call from a loon, squawking an alert to the other creatures at the lake. After all, there are no roads out here, none within 50 miles, and people are rare visitors.

"Look, up there!" my dad shouted, pointing toward shore. He had spotted a bald eagle stretching its six-foot wingspan. It glided, then spiraled down to a tree limb, its white tail feathers gleaming in the morning light.

"Things like this don't happen in Iowa," said my dad, now caught in his own childhood time machine, back in Iowa where he grew up.

Just then a tremendous strike on his rod brought us back to the present—Yow! A 20-inch rainbow trout did a pirouette on the lake surface, then sprinted off on a power run.

To clear the area, I began reeling my lure in, but—Yow!—I suddenly had one on my line as well, also a big one, and those two trout jumped like orcas on the Puget Sound. As we fought them, whooping at each surprise yank and jump, I remembered our first great fishing trip together, where we were catching fish on every drop, and how that helped make a demonic 12-year-old kid aware of the greatness that this world can offer.

Our rods were bent down like croquet hoops, and we finally coaxed the big trout to the boat. With quick swoops of the net, they were ours, both 20-inchers. They were wild rainbow trout, painted by nature with splotches of bright red on their cheeks and crimson stripes down each side, fish that had never known the feel of a hook until now.

This is how it is in the Canadian wilderness—lakes that can be reached only by float plane, big trout that worry about bald eagles instead of hooks, and the hooting of loons reverberating across the water, through your mind. It's a place where you find yourself remembering your days as a child, when you first started sensing how special the outdoors can be.

For hundreds of miles out here, there is nothing but woods and water. Hotnarko, Gatcho, Malaput, Petry, Fish, Eliguk—all lakes in divine settings. They are protected by high glacial-cut mountains to the east, and by a hostile climate that allows visitors only during summer. After a while here, you can get the feeling that this place will remain unspoiled to the end of time.

The same is true for the bonds among family. Given the right setting, they can last forever. For many, the great outdoors is the tie that binds.

❖

For a brochure, write Rainbow Lodge, Nimpo Lake, B.C., Canada VOL 1RO, or phone (604) 742-3252.

For information about Great Bear Lake, write Plummers' Great Bear Lake Lodges, 950 Bradford Street, Winnepeg, Manitoba, Canada R3H 0NS, or phone (800) 665-0240.

For information/brochures on Bowron Lakes Provincial Park, write D.J. Park Contractors, 358 Vaughan Street, Quesnel, B.C., Canada V2J 2T2. Phone (604) 992-3111 or fax (604) 992-6624.

INDEX

Index

THE AMERICAN HIKING SOCIETY AND THE AMERICAN DISCOVERY TRAIL

The American Discovery Trail, a brainchild of both the American Hiking Society and *Backpacker Magazine,* was turned from dream into reality on July 31, 1991 when the ADT scouting team completed a 14-month, 4,820-mile, coast-to-coast trek. (A significant portion of the hike crosses BLM lands across the West.) In 1993, a northern Midwest route was developed that includes Nebraska and Iowa and adds about 1,200 miles to the ADT. Congress passed legislation authorizing the National Park Service to conduct a feasibility study to determine if the ADT qualifies to be a National Scenic Trail. This study began in July 1993 and is expected to be completed by November 1995.

As in the early days of the Appalachian Trail (it took nearly half a century to finish that trail), the ADT follows dirt roads and quiet byways. Trail supporters hope to get much of the trail moved off-road, which will require the help of local hiking clubs and others committed to seeing the ADT blazed officially across mountains, forests and prairies.

A portion of the proceeds from this sale of *Epic Trips of the West* goes dierectly to the ADT. By purchasing this book, you have indirectly helped the American Hiking Society and all Americans realize the reality of a coast-to-coast trail. Want to do more? That's easy.

You can become an official part of the American Discovery Trail team by sending a $25 check (payable to the American Discovery Trail) to: American Discovery Trail, c/o American Hiking Society, P.O. Box 20160, Washington, DC 20041-2160. In return, you will receive official ADT updates, a subscription to *American Hiker* (the American Hiking Society's official publication), the American Hiking Society newsletter, and a free ADT decal.

NATIONAL TRAILS DAY

Scheduled to draw public attention to the National Trails System Act, the second annual National Trails Day (NTD) will unite all trail users, trail advocates, and the outdoor industry in a day of trails awareness nationwide.

"The goal of National Trails Day on June 4, 1994 is to make Americans more aware of the potential for developing and utilizing an interconnected and nationwide system of trails," states Bruce Ward, president of the American Hiking Society.

According to the American Hiking Society, 155 million people walk for pleasure; 93 million bicycle; 41 million hike; 43 million use trails for nature study, photography, small game hunting or primitive camping; 10 million ride horses on trails; five million backpack; and 11 million cross-country ski.

Through increased awareness and advocacy, it is hoped that a network of trails can be created nationwide that will provide all Americans access to local trails within 15 minutes of their homes. Cities such as Seattle, Miami, Missoula, Los Angeles, San Francisco and Portland, Maine have been active in creating such trail networks or greenbelts.

Getting involved with NTD is far more than just getting involved with a day of celebration, according to David Lillard, national director for NTD .

"I really see this as a kind of social revolution," says Lillard. "We are saying that trailways will bring together a wide range of community interests, including the needs of the community at large. By blurring the line between transportation and recreation, we are finding that trails are vital links between community facilities as well as between outdoor recreation areas."

The need for trails to become a critical part of a community's planning process is underscored by the fact that trail use is growing at an incredible rate. The U.S. Forest Service expects that day-hiking use will increase 93% over the next 50 years—incredible when you realize that presently, over 155 million Americans walk for pleasure.

The bottom line for ensuring long-term success instead of short-term sizzle, however, is the outdoor industry's and public's commitment to the national event and other similar events scheduled annually.

Kathleen Beamer, REI's public affairs director, sums up the importance of your participation this way: "(Public) involvement in trails and conservation ensures that places remain where people can escape to the outdoors and enjoy the solitude, challenge and beauty that makes this country so special."

The American Hiking Society, heavily behind the promotion and organization of this event, is ready to provide information about National Trails Day to everyone. Call (800) 972-8606.

WHAT IS THE NATIONAL TRAILS SYSTEM ACT?

Passed by Congress in 1968 to impart federal assistance to the Appalachian Trail and to help establish a national system of trails, the National Trails System Act provides for designation of approved trails as "national scenic trails" or "national historic trails." The Appalachian and Pacific Crest Trails were the first two trails to receive a "national scenic trail" designation.

The national scenic trail designation ensures continuous protected corridors for outdoor recreation. National historic trails recognize prominent past routes of exploration and military action. It is important to note that historic trails generally consist of remnant sites and segmented trails and are thereby not necessarily continuous. Although trails are protected by the government, land through which the trail travels may be either publicly or privately owned.